Me, the Crazy Woman, and Breast Cancer

Me, the Crazy Woman, and Breast Cancer

Strength and Inspiration for the Patient, Survivor, and Those Who Love Them

Stacy D. Shelton

Me, the Crazy Woman, and Breast Cancer
Strength and Inspiration for the Patient, Survivor, and Those Who Love Them
All Rights Reserved.
Copyright © 2009 Stacy D. Shelton
V2.0

Enlighten Press
A Division of Enlighten Communications, Inc., 805 Cedarbrook Drive, Norman, OK 73072

ISBN: 978-0-9825085-9-6

Library of Congress Control Number: 2009934022

PRINTED IN THE UNITED STATES OF AMERICA

For my daughter, Brealyn
Embrace all that is, and all that will be;
for life is about the journey.

Table of Contents

Absurd, amok, bananas, bats in the belfry, bonkers, cracked, cuckoo, daffy, demented, foolish, goofy, hare-brained, insane, loco, loony, maniac, nuts, psycho, senseless, strange, touched, unbalanced, wacky, weird.

That is the woman that lives inside my head and she won't shut up. From the moment she found out I had breast cancer, she has been a hemorrhoid on the butt of my life. She is ruthless — interfering with every single and sane thought that goes through my head.

I hate her.

But, mostly, I hate that as badly as I want her to be wrong; something tells me she's right. And that makes me hate her all the more.

Chapter One
Crazy Woman Arrives

There are few things that can comfort a woman who has been told she has breast cancer. In fact, everything she's known that once gave some form of comfort is rendered as useless as a microwave without electricity. At least that's the way it was for me.

I drove mindlessly home from the mammography center, not remembering any part of the trip, walked zombie-like into my kitchen, and went straight for the chocolate.

I unwrapped a Godiva when a shrill voice from inside my head screamed, "*Chocolate has caffeine, you moron! It has sugar too — poison. Those things are poison. You already have poison in your body. If you eat chocolate, you will be poisoning yourself even more. You can't have chocolate. Never again will you eat chocolate!*"

This was my introduction to the Crazy Woman who was

now living inside my head.

When you hear the words "You have cancer," time stands still. It plays with you like a bottle afloat in an angry sea of swirling, crashing waves. One moment, you think you are heading for shore, but the very next, you are knocked back into the torrential blackness.

It doesn't matter how hard you swim, the current is too strong. Then you realize it is only a matter of time before the sharks begin circling.

The illusion of control you thought you had over your life instantly dissolves. Like wiping steam from a mirror, you see clearly for the first time, that not only are you not in control of your life, you never were.

Logical thinking takes the next bus to Toledo. Every questionable decision you made in the past regarding how you treated your body comes flooding back.

"*If only I had exercised more. If only I hadn't used artificial sweeteners. I should have eaten more vegetables.*" It never ends.

I dropped the chocolate and walked into the small living room of a townhouse I had moved into a few weeks earlier. My husband and I had recently separated, and I and my fourteen-year-old daughter, Brealyn, had moved out.

Doug and I had been married seven years, most of them very difficult. We each brought an only child into the marriage, and it seemed that the obstacles in blending our families were almost too difficult to overcome.

Doug and I had very different parenting styles, and because both of our children were so young, they required our constant involvement.

That, in itself, was a recipe for failure, because Doug was gone all day, leaving me as the guardian. But I was a guardian with no authority. Oliver, my stepson, wasn't used to my type of parenting and needless to say, it wasn't effective. I loved Oliver, but common ground was hard to find, making it difficult to form a close bond with him.

On the other hand, Doug loved Brealyn, but she had an extremely close bond with her own father, leaving little to no room for another father figure.

In addition, because I was unsure of the marriage, I tried to keep them from getting too close. I didn't want her to be hurt if it didn't last.

Our worst problems, however, stemmed from Doug and me. Doug was an attorney, and I had run several successful businesses. We were both type A personalities — headstrong and committed to our own way. Compromise was not a common theme.

I became exhausted and I was tired of fighting a losing battle. We had made little progress throughout the course of our marriage, and the years had left us no closer to succeeding than when we began.

Doug also had a history of not being completely honest with me. I value honesty over everything else. I've always felt as if I didn't care what someone had to tell me — I could handle it. Just give me the respect of being honest.

Most of the lies were trivial. They were never deal break-ers, just "Don't tell her and she won't hassle me" stuff. But no matter how small the lie was, it sent me over the edge every time.

"Why can't you just be honest?" I pleaded. "What am I going to do, ground you?" It's a conversation we had re-peatedly — so much so that it never allowed us to build a foundation of trust.

Our issues with the children, the marriage, and his dis-honesty made me feel as if I was backed into a corner and I had to make a stand. I couldn't take it anymore. The bottom line was: I still loved him, but I could not live with him.

I walked into my living room and sank onto the couch. I turned on the television, watching it for about five seconds before turning it off again. I readjusted myself, subcon-sciously looking for a place where I would be comfortable. I roamed around the living room picking up objects and set-ting them back down again. The same question kept playing over again in my head. "How do I tell Brealyn?"

Brea, as we called her, was not a normal child of four-teen. She had the maturity of most forty-year-olds. But I was sure that when I told her the news, her façade would crumble back into that of a helpless child.

The thought of introducing my child to the mortality of her mother sent shivers up my spine. I imagined she would believe it to be a death sentence for me.

She was two when her father left me. Since that time, it

had been just the two of us until I remarried Doug five years later. Even after that, it always felt like us against them. We were the constants in each other's lives, and I believed that if she thought that was threatened, she would fall apart.

I continued my pacing, trying to form a way to tell her. I repeatedly played the conversation over in my head. Each time, it did not come out the way I wanted. When I got to the point where I said the word "cancer," I saw her falling to pieces; and I knew if she did, I would too.

"Okay," I told myself, *"Don't tell her yet. Wait until you know more about what you are dealing with."*

It was a plan I could live with except for one thing — my child could read me like a book. She always knew when something was wrong no matter how hard I tried to pretend it wasn't.

"You have to do this," I told myself. *"You can't scare her."*

The pacing had left me standing in the middle of my office. I looked around the room, wondering why I was there. A moment later, I reached for the phone and dialed my husband at work. When his receptionist answered the phone, I tried to sound extra cheery just to throw off any suspicion.

I realize now how needless that was. I don't think in her wildest dreams she would have suspected that I was calling Doug to tell him I had breast cancer.

When he answered the phone, I was surprisingly calm. "I just found out I have breast cancer," I said with no more emotion than if I had told him I had gotten a haircut.

"You have — oh my God — you have breast cancer?" he said, not believing his own words. "How? I mean, how do you know?"

I told him about my routine mammogram earlier that day and about the radiologist telling me he saw something he thought was cancer.

"He thought it was cancer, but he wasn't sure?" he asked, searching for a better scenario.

"No, I think he is pretty sure," I said. "He said something about calcifications and them being in a pattern that usually means it's cancer."

"I'll come over," he said. "I'll be there in twenty minutes."

I heard myself saying "Okay," before I really thought about it. When I hung up the phone, it occurred to me that I should handle the situation alone. But deep inside, I knew I needed him more than I have ever needed anyone.

The doorbell rang. I had been pacing only a couple of feet away, so I lunged to open it. Doug walked inside, pulled me close to his chest, and let out a sigh. "Tell me what happened," he said, holding me back so he could see my face. I motioned for him to follow me to the sofa, and I began recounting the afternoon.

"They made me wait a few minutes to make sure they had the images they wanted," I told him, replaying the moment in my head where I thought they would come back and tell me I could get dressed.

"But they told me they needed more pictures and I had to do it again. That's never happened before," I said. "I knew something was wrong. Plus I was getting upset, because it hurt more than usual this time."

I told him about the radiologist informing me he had found a small area that concerned him. I heard my voice speeding up to keep time with the beat of my heart.

"So I asked him if they found a lump, but he said no. Instead, I have calcifications in my milk ducts."

Doug looked at me, puzzled. I nodded my head in agreement.

"I was glad when he told me that, because I had trouble with my milk not drying up after Brea was born," I explained. "I figured it was just leftover, dried-up milk in there." Doug raised his eyebrows as if I were about to give him good news.

"So I told him just what I told you." I could see the relief on Doug's face. "But he looked at me as if I were stupid. He said that calcifications are usually a sign of breast cancer. He told me to see a surgeon right away."

Doug sat next to me in silence. I watched his face as he tried to grasp my new reality.

"Okay, we don't know for sure; so that's something. When are you seeing the surgeon?"

"Monday," I replied.

"I'll go with you," he said. I nodded.

He held me for several minutes. Finally, he rose, helping me up along with him.

"I want you to know I'm going to be here with you every step of the way," he said, looking me in the eye. He pulled me into him again, hugging me softly. "I've got to go," he said, "But I'll call you later."

I walked him to the door, and he leaned in and kissed me. Then he walked out my door and went to dinner with another woman.

Chapter Two
Betrayal

When Doug left, it was time for me to get Brea from school. I put on my extra-happy face when she got in the car.

"How was your day, Missy?" I asked. She rolled her eyes, mumbling something about same ole, same ole.

Much to my relief, when we got home, she went straight to her room. If she was around, I knew it would only be a matter of time before she sensed my preoccupation.

I busied myself with some paperwork, then I called Doug's house. I hadn't had enough time to let everyone know my new number, so I still checked the old one for messages. There was only one message, and it clearly was not meant for me.

"Hi, Doug," I heard a syrupy sweet female voice drawl. "I'm so excited that you asked me to have dinner with you tonight." I instantly recognized the voice as a woman that had pursued him when we had gone through a similar separation two years earlier. I became sick to my stomach as I listened to her flirt into the phone.

"Let's see, I want to tell you a little about my day," she bubbled. "It's been pretty easy so far…" I was about to collapse, but I continued to listen. My brain was like a transmission when a gas pedal gets stuck. It was roaring and retching, trying to make sense of what I had just discovered.

Doug and I had made an agreement that during this separation, we would not see other people. *"We've been apart for two weeks, and he's already going out with someone else?"* I asked myself, disbelievingly.

I hung up the phone and sank into my chair. I tried to digest the new information, wanting, in some way, to justify it.

"Okay, maybe he's just going out with a friend," I lied to myself. *"Maybe now that he knows I have cancer he's going to call and cancel,"* I reasoned. Brea called from upstairs, breaking into my excuses.

"Mom, I'm hungry, when are we going to eat?"

"No," I thought. *"I cannot handle making dinner."* I sighed and heard my mommy voice take over. "How about making it a pizza night?"

"YEAH!" she yelled, extremely happy that any night could be a pizza night.

I placed the order and then went to my bedroom to lie down. My head was swirling as I tried to process the last fifteen minutes of my life. I could feel my chest tightening, making it hard to breathe. "Just calm down," I said aloud. "There's got to be a good explanation for this." But deep inside I knew I was just fooling myself. I knew that it was really the beginning of the end.

I made it through the evening without breaking down. It was a heavy homework night, and Brea was a "hole up in her cave" kind of teen, so I didn't have to put on a brave face. I paced the floor, wondering if he was with her. At around nine, I couldn't stand it anymore.

"I'm going to run over to the house and pick up a few things," I yelled upstairs. I heard a grunt of acknowledgment and I left. The townhouse was only a few blocks away from Doug's, so the drive was short, giving me little time to concoct what I would say to him. When I got there, however, he wasn't home. I called his cell phone. "Hey, where are you?" I asked as if I knew absolutely nothing of where he was or with whom.

"Downtown," he answered.

"Downtown?" I asked innocently. "What are you doing downtown?"

"I was just having a drink," he replied.

"Yeah?" I said, sounding chipper. "Who are you having a drink with?" He hesitated. Doug was a terrible liar. I always caught him, because he had this way of hesitating, exactly as he had just done.

"Nobody," he finally said. "Just by myself."

"Oh, okay," I feigned. "Well, I'm here at the house. I

needed to grab a few things; but if you're downtown, I'll come by later."

He asked me to wait for him, telling me he was almost home.

"*Here we are again,*" I thought to myself as I waited for him. Doug's history of lying was repeating itself.

Soon, he pulled into the driveway and opened the garage door. I waved as he passed me, still playing it completely cool.

We walked into the kitchen and he settled himself on a barstool. "How are you doing?" he asked, concerned about my mental state since the news that afternoon.

"Oh, I don't want to talk about that," I brushed away the question with my hand. "How was your date?" I asked casually.

I might as well have punched him in the gut. Every ounce of blood drained from his face as he tried to swallow but couldn't. He had to take a deep breath and recover.

"I don't want to talk about her," he said, trying to downplay being caught.

I leaned into him and looked him squarely in the eye. "We are done." I picked up my purse and turned toward the door.

"Why?" he had the audacity to ask, and that just sealed the deal. The next morning, I called an attorney and began divorce proceedings.

***

I got in my car, and the screech I had heard that afternoon began again.

"Oh yeah, he wants to be there for you — when he's not out cheating!" Crazy Woman weighed in. I ignored her, trying to remain dignified. She was having none of that. All the way home, she plied me with how stupid I had been to think he could change.

"You are so predictable," she scolded. *"This is your own fault. Every time he lied to you, you let him. He's probably been seeing her all along, and you're such a pinhead, you didn't want to see it. Hell, his name could have been Pinocchio, and you still would have been clueless,"* she sneered.

As soon as I walked in the door, my phone was ringing. I knew it was Doug, so I didn't answer. The phone rang again. After about five calls, I dialed my voice mail. Each time he called, he left a message about how he wanted to be there for me. The more messages I heard, the angrier I got. At the same time, every message caused another piece of my heart to break.

In all my life, I had not been hurt like that. Maybe I could have dealt with it if the circumstances had been different. But, the fact that he walked out of my house after finding out I had cancer and straight to another woman was something that I could not wrap my mind around. Each time I tried, Crazy Woman would emerge.

"He never loved you. You are an idiot if you think he did,"

she told me. "*You've wasted the best part of your life living a lie. You need to wake up and smell the coffee, girlie.*"

As much as I wanted her to stop, I needed her to keep going. In my mind, I had told myself that I could live without him — that Brea and I could make it on our own, and that's why I moved out. I think I really believed that; but now, actually facing the end of my marriage, I could see how wrong I had been. My love for him was so deep and so strong that all I wanted was to pick up the phone, call him, and tell him we could work out something. I knew how pathetic it was, but I couldn't help it. I just wanted the pain to stop.

In retrospect, the devastation couldn't have come at a better time. This twist of fate helped to take some of my focus away from the cancer.

Throughout the weekend, I got more calls from him. Each time, the temptation to talk to him became greater. Finally, I blocked his number.

My friend, Laura, called on Sunday, which I knew was a setup from Doug. He knew that if anyone could get through to me, she could.

Laura had always been our biggest ally. She, being one of my closest friends, was consistently brought into the middle of our troubles. To complicate things, Doug also wanted her as his confidant. This created trouble between all of us, because to me, I had her first. How dare he horn in on my friend. She was supposed to be there for me one hundred percent of the time.

The problem was Laura's not like that. She calls them

as she sees them, and if I was the one in the wrong, she dutifully and tactfully told me so. This was a double-edged sword, because as much as I knew I needed someone to "get real" with me, I also needed someone to be just on my side, no matter what. I needed someone to curse him and call him a jerk, just because I thought he was.

She was ever the diplomat though, and I think it was because she was the one responsible for us getting together. She and Doug's best friend worked together, and the two thought we should go out. That blind date led to our marriage. I don't know if that is why she felt as if she had a personal stake in the relationship, but I do know that she was always the one to help get us back together when we had trouble.

"How are you?" she asked.

"I'm okay," I answered.

"Tell me what you've found out."

I told her everything I knew about the cancer. Her reply shocked me.

"I knew it. I knew it was only a matter of time."

"What do you mean?" I asked, dumbfounded. I had always known that I might get it because it appeared in my oldest sister at the age of thirty. But, I had been diligent about self-exams and mammograms. In fact, I had so many mammograms I was worried that the radiation from them would actually give me cancer. When I was thirty-eight, I told my OB/GYN that I was sick of having them.

"My lumps have never shown up on a mammogram. My sister's lump didn't show up. I think they are a total waste of time, and I've been having them for fourteen years. Enough is enough."

She said she felt it was okay for me to wait until I turned forty to have another one, and that's what I did.

"I don't know," Laura replied, snapping me back to our conversation. "I have just always had the feeling you would get it, and now you have."

That didn't make me feel any better, and it actually made me question if I might have given it to myself by thinking about it so much. I believe that thoughts are things, and we manifest into our lives the things on which we focus. Because I had worried about it since I was twenty-four, maybe I was the cause.

"You know, Stacy," she continued. You are going to need help. You are going to need someone to be by your side during this." I knew this was the part where she was going to try to get me back together with Doug — but, of course, he hadn't told her the whole story.

"Do you know that last week when I told him that I had cancer, he hugged me, looked me in the eye, and told me he would be here for me no matter what..."

"Of course, he did," she interrupted.

"Then he walked out the door and went out with another woman."

Long pause.

"He did what?" she was obviously taken aback. She knew the history between Doug and the woman, but now she acted as if I were making the whole thing up. "Are you sure?" she questioned.

I gave her a complete play-by-play of the night I found out.

"Well, screw him then!" she said, angrily. I exhaled. That was exactly what I needed to hear.

"I want to go with you to see your surgeon," she said.

"No, it's okay. I can do this. It's no big deal."

"Yes, it is. Let me go with you; that way, if you forget anything, I can remember to ask it."

"I've already got that covered. I made a list of everything I want to talk to her about. Really, it's okay. I'll be fine."

"Okay then, but I want you to call me the minute you get out of there. I want to know exactly what she says," she insisted.

"I will," I promised.

Chapter Three
Alone

Monday morning, I awoke to someone talking to me.
"You are going to die," Crazy Woman announced matter-of-factly.

I rubbed my eyes, trying to bring myself into consciousness. The night had been one of a tossing and fitful sleep. I had finally managed to collapse around five and slept until she arrived, about seven.

"You're going to die," she said again.

I looked around the room, still stupefied, until the grogginess left and I realized I was alone.

"Did you hear me?" she demanded. *"I said you're going to die."* I sat up.

"I'm not going to die," I retorted, not really knowing if the words rang true.

"Hah," she said, obviously privy to my insecurity. *"You*

don't really believe that. You think you are going to die."

"Shut up," I mumbled. "Just shut up. You don't know what you are talking about."

I threw back the comforter and put my feet on the floor. Thoughts about being strong and staying around to watch my daughter grow up began flooding my head.

"*I will not let this beat me,*" I assured her. "I can't and I won't," I said, sighing. I headed to the bathroom to shower so I could get my daughter to school.

When I returned home, the phone was ringing.

"I have found a really good surgeon for you if you're not comfortable with the one you're seeing." It was Laura. "This place is supposed to be top-notch for breast cancer," she added.

"Okay," I said. I felt as if I would be satisfied with the surgeon I was seeing that day, but I didn't know her, and I was skeptical because I was using someone from a small hospital. "Why don't we get an appointment, and if I don't feel comfortable after meeting with her, I'll go to the other." I was relieved that I wasn't going through this alone and that someone else had my back.

"I'll set up the appointment," she said.

"I'll call you after I meet with the surgeon," I told her, hanging up.

Later that afternoon, I returned to the same place I had the mammogram. The surgeon officed there part of the week.

A pleasant-looking young woman came into the exam

room and introduced herself as the doctor.

"I've looked at your slides," she said "and although we can't be sure until we biopsy the area, in cases like this, it usually turns out to be cancer. Now the good news is that it looks to be in the earliest possible stages. But the bad news is that it is so small, and it's so far against your chest wall that it's going to be hard to biopsy," she paused to see if I was understanding. "It's not a lump, just calcifications in your ducts, and those are hard to find. We may not get them unless we actually go in and do a partial mastectomy and just take out the whole area."

My head was swimming, and I had already forgotten everything I had wanted to ask her. I sat there for a moment trying to collect my thoughts, but I couldn't. She obviously sensed it and walked me through the rest of the conversation.

"If we biopsy it, we will just give you a local anesthetic and numb the breast. You'll lie on a table, face down, and we will go in with a long needle and try to pull out the cells. It will be uncomfortable, but it could save you from having surgery with general anesthesia," she explained.

I sighed, wincing at the idea of a long needle probing my breast.

"The other alternative is to go in and take it all out at once. That way, if the cells come back positive, it's already gone." She watched my face to see if I was still following her.

I didn't hesitate. "That's what I want to do. I want it out

now," I said.

"Okay, I notice you've already had two lumpectomies," she said looking at my chart. I explained that those had turned out to be no more than cysts.

"Well, this procedure will be a little different than those. With a lump, we know where to go. We can see it and tell how much tissue to take. This procedure is more difficult because it's encased, and we can't see it."

She explained that my breast would have to be compressed in the mammography machine while they threaded a long wire into it, wrapping it around the cancer.

"It's the only way we can see where I will need to take out the tissue," she apologized.

I felt all the blood rush from my face, and my head start to sway. Maybe this wasn't the option I wanted after all.

"I know that sounds bad," she continued, "but we'll give you a local, and you won't really feel it. Are you okay with that?" she questioned.

"I'm okay with it," I answered reluctantly, although I wasn't.

We scheduled the surgery for about ten days later. As I left, the nurse gave me stacks of paperwork and told me she would schedule my pre-op tests.

I walked out of the hospital and called Laura.

"I think I'm going to use this surgeon," I told her. "I feel comfortable with her, and she can do the surgery next week."

"Are you sure?" she asked.

"Yeah, I'm sure. I just want this over. If things don't go right, I'll switch. But I think she's going to be fine." I hesitated, unsure of my next move. I hadn't really thought about all the ramifications of not having a husband around to help me, but I knew I couldn't ask Doug to take me to the surgery. Just the thought of even being around him filled me with enough rage and hurt to take me to my knees.

"Is there any way you might be able to take me to the surgery and back home?" I was ashamed to ask. Laura was a single mom who worked full time. I knew she didn't have the time to babysit me.

"Of course I will," she said. "It's no big deal for me to get off work, and I can stay with you the whole day." I felt a small weight lift from my shoulders. Now all that was left to do was to tell Brea and my family. I dreaded that more than the surgery.

"Thanks. I really appreciate this." I started tearing up, and she could tell.

"It's going to be okay," she soothed. "You are going to beat this. It's the best prognosis you could get." I could hear her searching for more words of comfort, but I just needed to retreat into my own world.

"I'll call you later with all the details," I said.

Chapter Four
Breaking the News

On the way home from the appointment, I called my mother to tell her the news. I downplayed everything as much as I could.

"You don't need to come — it's just an outpatient thing, and Laura is going with me."

"Laura? What about Doug?" she asked.

"He's seeing someone else and I don't want him there." She could tell from my voice that I was not going to discuss the subject with her.

"I don't mind coming...," she added.

"Really, it's no big deal. It'll be over in an hour, so there's no need."

I could tell she wanted to come, but our relationship had been strained for many years. I found it hard to be around her, and I knew her presence would only add to my anxiety.

"If you're sure…," she acquiesced.

I drove home and walked into the house, not knowing what to do with myself. I called other friends, told them the news, and went through the same "It's not a big deal" spiel. I told them not to mention it around Brea yet because I hadn't told her.

I was still struggling with how to tell her, but I knew I was out of time. I played the conversation over in my head the rest of the afternoon until it was time to pick her up from school.

"Hey, you want to stop and get an Icee?" I asked when she bounded into the car. I could tell she was in a good mood and I was glad. I wasn't looking forward to having this conversation with a sullen teen.

"Yeah!" she said excitedly.

We stopped at a convenience store a short distance from her school. Many of the kids stopped there for after-school snacks. I watched as she hugged her friends, acting as if she hadn't seen them in ages, although they had just left each other.

Her generation was so much more affectionate than my friends and I had been. They always told each other they loved them. They hugged and wrestled and played. I watched her, thinking to myself, "*I hope she will always be this way. I hope what I'm about to tell her doesn't change her.*"

When we got home and she dropped her backpack on the floor, I stopped her before she went upstairs.

"Brea, I need to talk to you a moment," I said, motioning for her to come sit by me.

"What did I do now?" she said, rolling her eyes. I laughed.

"You didn't do anything, weirdo. I just need to tell you a couple of things that are going to happen in the next week."

"What?"

"Well, I've got to have a little surgery next week." Surgeries were not a big deal to her. I had already had both of my hips replaced in the past two years, and although she panicked on the first one, by the second time, she acted as if I was just having a tooth pulled.

"Is something wrong with your hip?" she asked as she slurped her drink.

"No, I had a mammogram last week, and they found a little place that they want to take out. They think it may be cancer, but they found it at the best possible time. It's no big deal, and I'll be home the same day."

"Okay," she said getting up from the sofa. "It will be okay, Mum Mum," she said, patting me on the head. Then she turned and bounded up the stairs. "I'm going to do my homework," she called down.

I continued to sit there, my mouth hanging open. While I had envisioned this talk going a hundred different ways, this had not been one of them.

"Close your mouth, dummy," I heard Crazy Woman say. *"That's what you wanted, wasn't it — for her not to be worried? Well, she's not worried. Pat yourself on the back."*

I had done it. She hadn't fallen apart — far from it. I hadn't fallen apart. *"I'm good,"* I told myself, and I breathed for the first time in days.

The phone rang, and I was hoping it wasn't anyone calling to talk about the news. The few friends I had told had a serious grapevine, and the last thing I wanted was to re-explain everything.

"Hello," I said wearily.

"Stacy, don't hang up." It was Doug.

"Damn," I thought, I had forgotten to block his work number.

"What, Doug?" I tried to sound as put out as I possibly could.

"Baby, I really wish you would let me be there with you," he pleaded.

"Go be with your girlfriend," I retorted.

"She is just a friend. We just had dinner," he tried reasoning.

"Then why did you need to lie about it?" I seethed.

"I don't know. I'm sorry. I knew you would get upset, and I didn't want to upset you with everything you are going through."

"And you didn't think it would upset me for you to go out with her to begin with?" My voice was getting higher pitched with each word.

"Please just tell me what the doctor said today," he begged.

"That's none of your business," I said angrily.

"Please, just let me help you."

"You've done enough," I said, and I hung up the phone, immediately blocking the number.

During the next few days, I tried to keep my life as normal as possible. My diagnosis came two weeks after I kicked off my tenth season as a softball coach. I had coached Brea in softball since she was four years old, playing T-Ball. Most of the girls I coached at the time had been with me since they were in second grade. At our next practice, it was obvious they had been told about my cancer.

The news caused a change in them. They wouldn't look at me when I talked to them. They didn't kid around and goof with each other or me as much as before. So at the following practice, I brought them around me in a circle.

"I know you guys have heard I have breast cancer," I said, looking for facial expressions that would tell me how I should continue. Every eye hit the ground, confirming their discomfort.

"Well, I want you to know everything is fine," I said so convincingly I believed it myself.

"I am going to have a quick surgery, and then I'll be right back out here with you guys." Eyes began to lift.

"We found it at the best possible time, so I don't have to do anything other than have it removed," I continued.

All eyes were now on me.

"And I want you to know that I don't want you to feel as

if you can't talk to me about it."

Feet began shuffling.

"I don't want you to feel weird or think you can't ask me questions."

Eyes began lowering again.

"Okay, out on the field," I said, taking the cue that the last thing they wanted to do was talk to me about it.

Backs turned and chatter ensued. They were going to be okay. In fact, nothing was ever mentioned again, and the season continued as the past nine before. I scolded and they rolled their eyes. I coached and they absorbed. We had a great time. Me, mostly because I had something in my life that wasn't about me, and them, mostly because they had something in their life that was about them — the way it should be.

Chapter Five
Facing My Demons

I held myself together masterfully until the following weekend. Friday night, I was alone because Brea had gone to her father's for the weekend. There was only quiet around me, giving me nothing to do but face my demons and Crazy Woman, who was the worst demon of all.

As I lay in bed, she began to hiss, *"You are going to die."* I refused to acknowledge her.

"You are going to die," she hissed again. Then again. And again.

My heart began to race. I was finding it hard to breathe. During the past week, I had gone into control mode. Take control of the situation. Take control of my daughter's feelings. Take control of my friends' worries. It left little time to actually comprehend what I was facing, and it now wanted acknowledgment.

I started feeling as if I really was going to die, not from the cancer, but from a heart attack. I could feel blood rushing to my head. I was dizzy; my heart was beating out of my chest. I began to panic and didn't know what to do. Before I could think rationally, I picked up the phone and called Doug.

"I need to come over," I started crying.

He sounded shocked that I had called him. How he replied, though, shocked me even more.

"I don't think that's a good idea."

I tried to process his response. He had been calling and emailing me continuously asking to "be there," and now he was telling me no. I finally rationalized that he thought I was coming over to fight.

"Look, I don't even know why I'm calling you." I could barely sit up without feeling as if I would faint. "I just can't be alone right now. I feel like I'm having a nervous breakdown."

He was silent.

"I'll sleep in the guestroom. Just don't make me stay here by myself," I pleaded.

"Okay," he agreed. "Come on over."

I packed my toothbrush and drove over in my pajamas. When I got there, he let me in, and I collapsed into him.

"What's wrong?" he asked, stroking my hair.

"I'm just freaking out," I replied. "Thanks for letting me come over."

"It's okay," he soothed. "It's going to be okay."

"I know."

I went to the guest room and got into bed. He followed me.

"You don't have to sleep in here," he said.

"I think it's for the best. I just needed to get out of my house." I tried not to sound as if I was crazy. "I'll just stay here tonight, and I'll be better in the morning."

"Okay," he reluctantly replied. "Yell if you need me." He then turned off the light and closed the door.

I felt better, and I willed the voice not to return, finally falling asleep.

The next night, I was at home and the same thing happened again. I felt like an elephant was on my chest. No matter how hard I tried to breathe, it was as if I could not fill my lungs.

"*You are going to die,*" she taunted.

"*Shut up,*" I told her. "*I'm not going to die.*"

I tried to change positions on the bed.

"*Yes, you are,*" she singsonged.

I tried reasoning with her. "*We caught it early; it's not a big deal.*"

"*You don't know that.*"

"I do!" I yelled.

I called Doug again but got no answer. It was around nine, and I wondered where he could be. I got up to turn on the television and try to escape the maddening voice. I flipped through channel after channel, but nothing could stop it.

I called again. No answer.

Fifteen minutes went by. No answer.

This went on for another hour. My brain then went into overdrive. *"Where is he?"* I kept asking myself.

"He's with her," Crazy Woman chimed in.

"No, he's not. He wouldn't do that," I tried convincing her.

I paced the floor. I went into every room of the house. I went upstairs into Brea's room and lay on her bed, smelling her pillows and trying to make myself feel as if I wasn't all alone.

At midnight, I called again. No answer. I called his cell phone. No answer. I called the house again. No answer.

"I told you," she said smugly. *"He's with her again."*

I got into some shorts and a T-shirt and drove to his house. I could tell he wasn't there, because there were no lights on, but I got out anyway and rang the doorbell. It had begun misting rain, and I stood at the doorway shivering. No answer.

I decided that I was going to let myself into the house. If he was seeing her, I was going to find out. I went through the gate and into the backyard. It was very dark, but I had hidden an extra key in our shed in case Brealyn had ever locked herself out.

I opened the door and reached above the two-by-four framing it. The key wasn't there. *"That's impossible,"* I thought. *"Doug didn't even know it was here."* I searched the rest of the shed, but to no avail. Finally, I gave up and walked to the patio where I saw a faint light coming from the master bedroom. The blinds were closed, but I could barely see through a small crack. A lamp on the nightstand was on, but the bed was made and it was clear he wasn't home.

I sat down on a patio chair as the rain began coming down harder. I scooted back under the awning so it wouldn't hit me. It was one in the morning by then. "*Where is he?*" I kept asking myself.

"*You know where he is,*" Crazy Woman chided.

I refused to acknowledge her. "*He'll be here any moment,*" I told myself and I waited. Each time I heard a car in the neighborhood, I convinced myself it was him coming home. By two, I was freezing and I was crying.

"*Maybe he went out of town with friends,*" I began telling myself. "*That's it,*" I sighed. "*He's just at the lake or something.*" I wrapped my arms around myself and ran through the rain back to my car. I drove home and got back into my pajamas. I tried to sleep but couldn't. At three, I picked up the phone and called him again.

"Hello," he sounded groggy. I was in shock. I had really managed to convince myself that he was gone and not with her.

"Where have you been?" I heard my voice screech.

"I've been here," he replied.

"No, you haven't!" I yelled. "I was there. You were not at home. I was there until after two. Where were you?" I demanded.

"I'm sleeping; let me talk to you in the morning," he whispered.

"No, Doug, I need to come over now."

"No. I don't want you to do that," he said. "Go to sleep and we'll talk in the morning."

"I can't sleep. I've been freaking out again. I need to come over there," I pleaded pathetically.

"No, you can't," he said.

"Is someone with you? You're not by yourself are you? Is that why I can't come?" I was becoming hysterical.

"No, there's nobody with me," he sounded perturbed. "Look, I'm really tired. I was out late, and now you and I both need to get some sleep."

"Why won't you tell me where you've been?" I demanded.

"Because it's none of your business," he responded.

I was stunned.

"What do you mean it's none of my business?"

"We agreed that we were going to take some time off and see where we want to go," he said. "You can't try and keep tabs on me all the time."

I knew right then he had been with her, and I also knew he wasn't going to admit it. I felt like I was going to throw up. Every part of my being was burning, and my heart was about to explode.

"You've been with her again!" I started crying. "Haven't you?"

"I'm not going to have this conversation with you," he

said. "I'm going to bed."

"If you weren't with her, why don't you just say so," I begged, hoping upon hope that he would do so.

"I'm not going to tell you where I was, because it's none of your business — not because I was with someone else. I'm going to bed. I'll talk to you in the morning," and he hung up.

I paced the floor the rest of the night. I was so mad, hurt, and confused all at once. Part of me kept telling myself he was out with friends, and he was just trying to make me jealous. Crazy Woman was having none of that. *"He's been with her, and you are just too stupid and too pathetic to admit it."*

I sank down on my bed and sobbed.

"You are the most pathetic person I've ever seen," she continued. *"You tell him you don't want to see him because he lies to you, and then you go and throw yourself at him. Pathetic!"* she roared.

I continued sobbing, partly because I had just witnessed the final nail in the coffin of my marriage, but mostly because I knew Crazy Woman was right.

After that, I couldn't stand the thought of Doug. Every time he popped into my mind, I got sick. The worst of it was that he was popping into my mind constantly. I went to the video store and rented as many movies as I could get my hands on in order to escape the thoughts.

Two days later, he emailed — again asking me to let him

come to my surgery. I never replied. I also made sure Laura knew what had happened so he would no longer have an ally in her. In my mind, I had never been more through with a relationship than I was then. The idea that he even had the gall to ask to be with me made me want to hit something.

Chapter Six
The Epiphany

Laura picked me up very early Thursday morning. I had arranged for my friend Ann to take Brea to school and bring her home.

I checked in, put on a gown, and after a nurse put in an IV, I was taken to the mammography center.

"Ms. Shelton," a middle-aged nurse greeted me. "I know the doctor has gone over the procedure we are about to do with you, but I want to go over it again with you in case you have any questions."

I nodded my head.

"You are going to have to be standing up for this, so if you get queasy or feel faint, you'll need to let us know right away." She looked at me, concerned. "First, we are going to numb your breast. Then we will insert it into the mammography machine," she said pointing to it. "When we have you set, I'm going to insert this wire into your breast and thread it around the area that the surgeon needs to take out." I could feel the blood draining from my face. "The radiologist will be over there watching the screen and directing me which way to go," she said, motioning to a computer screen adjacent to the mammography machine. "When we get it done, we'll take you back to pre-op, and then you'll have the surgery. Do you have any questions?" she asked.

"No."

"Okay, then let's get started."

My breast stung as they injected me with the numbing medicine. I winced. "Are you okay?" the nurse asked.

I shook my head yes.

"Okay, come stand over here and face me," she said as she navigated me to the mammography machine.

She placed my breast on the cold plastic and began pulling my chest into it.

"This may be uncomfortable because we have to get as close to your chest wall as we can. Your ribs may get a little sore," she cautioned.

As the machine began to compress my tissue, I could feel my skin pulling and stretching. I remembered that people pass out if they don't bend their knees, and since I was prone to passing out, I bent them.

"Okay, here comes the wire," she warned.

I looked away. I felt a small prick and tugging. Then I felt something sharp rip through my tissue.

"Ow," I heard myself say.

"Does that hurt?" she asked, confused.

"Yeah, it does," I winced again.

"I'm sorry, the anesthetic must have not have taken effect yet," she apologized. "Just hang on, we're almost there."

She looked up at the radiologist.

"About two more centimeters," he nodded.

The room began to fade.

"I'm going to pass out," I told her breathlessly.

Fainting was an irritating habit that I had since I was a child. If I even got the flu, I would drop like a lead balloon.

"Oh no, no, no," she said, dropping the wire, which now lay hanging out of my breast and down my side.

She raced around to the back of me at the same time the radiologist raced to my side. He grabbed me under my left arm; she grabbed my waist.

"Take a deep breath, and close your eyes," she said. She was using her foot to pull a tall, adjustable chair toward me. "I can't let you out of the machine, but I'm going to put this under your butt, and you can sit," she said frantically. "Keep breathing in through your nose and out through your mouth."

I felt the chair slide beneath me, and I sat down as well as I could without pulling the skin on my breast.

I sat there a couple of minutes until the dizziness had passed.

"I'm okay," I told them. "I'm sorry."

"It's okay — happens all the time," the nurse responded. "Is it okay for us to continue? We're almost done."

I nodded again, and they both resumed their places. After a few more minutes of using each other to get the wire placed, she raised the compression plate.

"All done," she chirped. "I think we'll take you back in a wheelchair though, just to be safe."

"Good idea," I murmured as she handed me off to an aide who wheeled me back to my waiting room in pre-op.

I lay on the bed looking at the wire as it hung from my side. The thought that it was in me started making me queasy. My breast hurt, throbbing a little, but it didn't hurt as badly as the hole in my heart.

I couldn't believe I was at the hospital going through this surgery without my husband or my daughter.

I lay on the gurney waiting and feeling like I was having an out-of-body experience. The curtain opened and a nurse stuck her head inside.

"We are running a little behind," she apologized. "It's probably going to be another half hour, so why don't you try and get some rest."

"Okay," I responded, knowing there was no way I was going to get any rest.

As I lay there staring at the curtain for another hour, I looked back on my life with Doug. I was so devastated at the events of the last weeks. Each thought of him made me lose my breath. I wanted to scream and kick and cry and throw something. Mentally, I just could not understand any of it.

"Why do you care?"

Crazy Woman had decided to make an appearance.

"You left him. You told him you couldn't live with him anymore, and now you want to sit around and act like a victim? Poor pitiful Stacy — she's so mistreated," she chided.

I tried to ignore her, but the question wouldn't release its hold until I finally acknowledged it. *"Why do I care?"* I silently wondered, but the answer was obvious. No matter what he had done, I was still in love with him. I no more wanted my marriage over than I wanted another hip replacement.

The more I thought about our marriage, the more apparent it became as the past seven years of our life came flooding back to me. I saw every single thing that I had done to ensure that the marriage would fail. I had spent the entire time blaming him for all our problems, but when I looked at it — really looked at it — I had to carry the burden of more of our problems than I had been willing to own. I realized that I had been repeating a pattern I had seen my whole life.

I was raised with an alcoholic father. He was a mean drunk, and he lived every second of every day angry. I watched as he and my mother battled to the brink of death on many occasions.

I lived my entire childhood in horrible fear of the man. Our lives were in constant turmoil. I was diagnosed with my first ulcer at ten years of age. I dreaded being at home, and by the time I was in high school, I was in every activity the school offered so I did not have to be there.

My teachers thought I was driven and set on being successful, but in reality, I was afraid I might die or that I might witness my mother or siblings die if I was at home. So, I stayed away as much as I possibly could.

Lying on that gurney, my first marriage came back to me too. My ex-husband had treated me like a queen. I remember a friend of mine saying to me one time, as if he pitied him, "Bless his heart, he worships the ground you walk on, and you act like you could care less." I laughed about it then, but I wasn't laughing now. It was very clear at that moment that I had been carrying around the same anger that my father had nursed for as long as I had known him.

Why was I angry? Why did I need to assault the people I loved? I surmised that it was because that is all I had ever known. My father never tried to resolve an issue peacefully. His only mode of communication had been to scream, yell, curse, and attack.

I heard the words ring in my head. *"Life is too short."*

For the first time in my life, I realized how true that statement was. I might not be around in a year. Did I really want to spend whatever time I had left angry and acting like my father had? The answer was, absolutely, no. I despised everything he had done to our family. I hated everything he had stood for then.

"Then grow your ass up and change," Crazy Woman scolded.

"I will," I shamefully acknowledged.

***

"Ms. Shelton, are you ready?" a nurse came into the cubicle. "Sorry it took so long."

I nodded my head yes, although it was still swimming with the newfound realizations. I lay flat on the gurney as the nurse pushed me through a white sterile hall. I watched the ceiling tiles pass, one after the other, trying to keep from thinking about what lay ahead. Each tile brought the fear and the surgical room closer. I began counting them to keep the nervousness at bay. She pushed the gurney through two swinging doors.

I saw nurses in blue scrubs, hairnets, and masks scurrying throughout the surgical room. The attending nurse pushed my gurney next to the operating table and the other nurses helped lift me onto the cold surface. I lay back, looking up again, but this time into the face of the anesthesiologist. He looked down upon me and placed a mask over my face. "Breathe and count backwards from ten," he said.

I began counting, "*ten...nine...eight...*"

"Can you wake up for a moment?" I heard a female voice ask. I blinked into semi-consciousness, looking around for something familiar. "Stacy, you did really well," I heard the surgeon say. "I think we got it all. We are going to send everything to pathology, and then we'll know more. Call my office tomorrow and set up an appointment for one week," she said.

"Umm," I heard myself answer as I drifted back into blackness.

Chapter Seven
Ducks With Carcinoma

The following week, I saw the surgeon for my post-op checkup. She walked into the room where I was seated on the exam table and sighed loudly.

"We got the test results back on the tissue we removed," she said as she leaned against the supply cabinet.

"You have ductal carcinoma in situ."

I heard "Ducks with carcinoma inside you."

My blank stare told her to repeat it.

"Ductal carcinoma in situ," she said more slowly, making sure I heard each word.

Crazy Woman began yelling inside my head, *"Who gives a flying flip what it's called?"* I, on the other hand, calmly asked, "What does that mean?"

"Really, it's exactly what we thought it was. It means there are or were cancerous calcifications in your milk ducts," she said. "The good news is we got this at the earliest possible stage. There was no metastasis."

"It hasn't spread?" I asked, trying to clarify.

"Exactly. It is — was — all inside the ducts, and the report says we got clean margins."

"What does that mean — clean margins?"

"I took out enough extra tissue to make sure there was nothing else there," she said, making a round circle with her thumb and forefinger. "I took out about a golf-ball-size area. The edges came back clean of cancer; so we got it all."

I sighed. "Thank God."

"We still need to talk about treatment options," she said.

"*You're going to be bald!*" Crazy Woman screamed.

"You mean chemo?" I asked, taking my cue from Crazy Woman.

"No," she replied. I silently said a "*Ha!*" to Crazy Woman.

"It wasn't invasive, so you don't have to have chemotherapy," she continued. "But we might want to consider radiation treatments, and there is a drug called tamoxifen that we use to help stop the production of the hormones that feed the cancer. By the way, yours was estrogen and progesterone positive."

I flinched at the way she said "yours," as if it was something I owned. The last thing I wanted to do was lay claim to this traitor that had inhabited my body.

"I don't understand," I told her.

"It means that the cancer feeds off estrogen and progesterone."

"Really?" I asked, confused.

I had gotten a hormone saliva test two months earlier, and it had revealed that I had no progesterone in my body. It also said I had an over abundance of estrogen. What she was saying didn't make sense.

"I know it's confusing, but if you didn't have the progesterone, then it was feeding off just the estrogen. If you had progesterone, it would have fed off that too," she explained.

My brain became mush. I didn't really understand anything she was telling me. It almost sounded like a McDonald's drive-thru. "I'll have a large estrogen with a side of progesterone, please. Oh yeah, and a Diet Coke."

I thought some more about what she had said to me. I knew I didn't want to go back to feeling the way I had before I took the progesterone. I had been tired, moody, gaining weight for no reason. The bio-identical progesterone cream had made all that disappear. I thought it was a godsend.

"I would like to stay on the progesterone. I've done a lot of research on hormones, and I think it is just as bad to have too little as it is to have too much," I told her.

She looked perplexed as if she didn't like what I was saying, but she couldn't argue with it either. I took that as a green light and continued my list of what I wanted to do.

"I don't want to take tamoxifen either. I think it's a poison, and I don't want another poison in my body. I don't know a lot about it, but I just don't feel like it's the right option for me." I searched her face for a sign that she was getting upset with me directing my own course of care. There was none.

"That's okay," she said. "It's not mandatory, and since we caught yours so early, I think that's reasonable. You are going to have to have mammograms every six months now though…"

I interrupted. "Don't you think too many mammograms will give me too much radiation?"

"No." She was very firm about this. "There is so little radiation in the mammograms that it will not have that kind of effect," she paused, looking again at my chart. "What about the radiation treatments?" she asked.

"You are telling me that I had a stage zero form of cancer and that you got all of it and that I have clean margins," I parroted back to her. "Tell me what radiation will do for me?"

"If there are any stray cells…," she began, but again I interrupted her.

"You said they were inside my ducts. How can they be stray?"

"Well, at this point, I don't really think they could. And, if you have radiation…," she was beginning to think aloud, "and the cancer comes back, it limits what treatment options we have then."

"How so?"

"You can't have radiation twice. Even if it wasn't metastasizing, you would still probably have to have a total mastectomy just to be safe."

That was all I needed to hear.

"I don't want the radiation then," I blurted.

"Okay, then you will just come back in six months, and we will do another mammogram and make sure everything is okay." She stuck her hand out to shake mine.

"Thank you so much," I told her, gratefully. "I really appreciate everything you've done."

"You're welcome. I'll see you in six months," she reiterated, as she left the room.

I sat there for a moment questioning my decisions. They felt good. I felt like I had control again over my life. Who knew cancer could be this easy?

Chapter Eight
The Confession

I was fortunate in that I owned a home-based business and I could work whatever hours suited me — or not at all if the situation called for it. For the next few days, I lay around watching movies and recuperating. I could feel the anesthesia was still in my body and keeping me sluggish and tired. Friends called to check on me, brought food, and shuttled Brealyn to and from school. I felt blessed.

Doug had begun emailing me, again telling me he wanted to be there for me and asking that I let him know what the doctors said.

I was struggling with how to reopen our relationship and if it was really a good idea to do so. My epiphany had been playing through my head for days. I knew the change in my own psyche wouldn't be enough to completely fix our relationship. I was not the only one who needed to change.

Doug also had a temper and was used to being in control. I was never a person anyone could control. I knew by the peace that had come over me that I was changed. I was resolved, now that I had identified the problem, that I would never live that way again. The question was, could we have the kind of relationship that was trusting, functional, and peaceful if we were together?

I waited a few more days before I responded to the mail. I had to look at what my newfound knowledge could realistically do for the relationship. I wanted to be sure that the "new me" would make enough of a difference to justify trying again.

I went back through many of the very trying scenarios we had during our relationship and asked myself if I would have handled them differently, would the outcome have been different? Most of the time, the answer was yes.

I wasn't going to take responsibility for Doug's actions, and I didn't believe that I could change him. He was going to have to want to change. The changes I wanted to see in him, such as honesty, had to be things he wanted for himself, but I also knew that it was the one thing I had to have in order to be happy. If he lied to me about even the smallest thing, I wouldn't be able to get past it — I knew this — and I knew we would be right back where we had started.

I decided I needed to have a real conversation with him about what he did and did not want in his life before I could even begin to look at us together again. I picked up the phone and called him.

"Hello," he answered before the first ring ended, and I could tell he was fumbling to get the phone to his ear. It was clear he had been waiting for me to call.

"Doug, we need to talk," I said cautiously.

"I know, baby," he replied. "I've been so worried about you. I'm so glad you called. I need you to know how much I care about you. I've been sick," he sounded as if he was choking back tears. "Laura told me about the surgery. I can't believe you wouldn't let me be there. I still want to be your friend, if nothing else."

"I appreciate that, but I can't be friends with someone who lies to me," I countered.

"I know," he said weakly. "I'm so sorry."

"I don't really want to talk about this right now," I said. "But I would like to talk to you soon. We need to get some things straightened out. My attorney has some questions we need to talk about too."

He sighed. I could tell he didn't want to talk about attorneys, and I really hadn't meant to bring that up either, but part of me wanted to save face and not let him think he was getting off easily.

"I can come over later," he said tentatively.

"How about we talk tomorrow? Brea is here now, and I don't want to feel stifled. We need to be able to talk openly," I added. "Can you go to work a little late and come by here first?"

"Yeah, I think I can do that," he said.

"Okay, I'll see you then." I started to hang up the phone.

"Baby?"

"Yeah?"

"I love you."

"I'll see you tomorrow," I said, finding it too hard to push the hurt back enough that I could say those words to him again.

The following morning, Doug arrived as promised. He was in a suit and tie, which meant he had either a client meeting or a court appearance. I knew I was at a disadvantage when I saw him, because I loved the way he looked in his tailored suits.

I was drinking coffee, and he had brought with him a cappuccino. He looked as wary as I did. We exchanged pleasantries, and I motioned for him to follow me into the living room. I awkwardly reached for the remote to turn off the morning news, trying to buy some time to get into the mindset of our pending conversation. When the television was off, I turned to him.

"I really don't know how to start this," I hesitated. "I'm unsure what to say, and I'm unsure if I really want to say it." I looked him in the eye.

"It's unbelievable to me that you went out with another woman on the day you found out I had cancer." I almost choked on the words.

"So it is cancer then?" he asked, ignoring the statement.

"Yes, it was," I countered. He began shaking his head back and forth.

"I can't believe it." He grabbed my hand. "Will you please tell me what you know?" he pleaded.

"I will, but I'd like to get back to our conversation." I was getting irritated, because I felt that the pity was just an attempt to deflect his indiscretions. Doug was an unbelievable attorney, and one of his assets was that he could deflect, redirect, manipulate, and completely discombobulate a subject that wasn't advantageous to him.

He looked down sadly. I realized he hadn't been trying to avoid the subject but was genuinely worried about me.

"I'm fine and everything is going to be fine," I told him the short version so we could get on to the matters at hand. "Doug, I don't think you are ever going to know what this has done to me," I said, pulling my hand away.

"I want you to know that nothing happened; we are just friends and I wanted to have dinner with someone. I was mad because you had not been taking my calls. I know it's stupid, but I felt justified."

This was not what I wanted to hear, and it was not making it any easier to "turn the other cheek."

"Doug, you lied to me *again*." I could feel the heat rising in my face. "I can't really believe you are going to tell me you were justified."

"Wait a minute," he cautioned. "I didn't say I was justified. I wasn't — I know that. I said I felt justified at the time."

"That doesn't make it any better," I said. "One of the biggest problems in this marriage — the biggest problem for me was your dishonesty. I have to have honesty first and foremost, above everything else." I was getting tense knowing I had already had this same conversation with him a million times. I felt like I was falling into the same hole I had been falling into for seven years. A feeling of helplessness came over me. I believed it would end the same way it always had, with his standard "I'll try and do better" bandage, which would temporarily close the wound, until the next time he couldn't be truthful.

He surprised me.

"I don't want to lie to you. I don't know why I do it. I hate conflict with you."

"Do you not understand that lying causes even more conflict?" I asked, shaking my head in a "duh" kind of way.

"I know it does, and at the time, all I want to do is to stop another argument — so I tell you what you want to hear."

This was the first time I had ever heard him acknowledge openly that it was a problem for him too.

"That's why I wanted to talk to you," I got up from the couch, trying to find a way to tell him what I had discovered while waiting for my surgery. I knew how cliché it would sound to tell him I had an epiphany.

"I don't want this to sound dumb," I hedged. "But while I was about to have surgery, I had a lot of time to think," I continued searching for the right words, but they weren't coming.

"This is going to sound absurd," I hedged again. "I…" It was like pulling a tooth — I knew it needed to come out, but I was terrified I would be making a huge mistake by telling him. I was about to give him the upper hand, and I didn't want him to think I was weak — that he could just get by with anything and I would forgive him. But I had to tell him, even if it meant making myself vulnerable all over again.

When I could stall no longer, I resigned to just saying it, cliché and all.

"I had an epiphany, and…" I paused again. "I don't want a divorce," I blurted out, and then I immediately crumbled, tears gushing down my cheeks. I sat down again to steady myself.

I saw a look of shock and relief on his face. Then came the doubt.

"I know," I acknowledged his trepidation. "I know I said it was a done deal. I know I already filed for it, and I don't know how to explain it other than to tell you that I realized what I've done to hurt our marriage — that it wasn't just you. I don't want to be like that anymore. I can't. Life is too short." I heard the words ringing like they had rung in my head the day of my surgery.

"What do you mean?" he asked. "What have you done to hurt the marriage?" I could tell he had gone into lawyer mode and was trying to coerce a total confession from me — to set me up. I had to stop myself from being caught up in the game of cat and mouse, at which we were both fiendishly good. I had to be honest and stop the games.

"Doug, I know I have an anger problem." I was having problems wiping away the tears fast enough before they streaked my face again. I walked to the bathroom to get a tissue.

"Wait! Don't walk off," he begged. He knew he was about to get everything he wanted.

I threw up a finger, motioning for him to wait a minute. I got a tissue and came back into the room. He had a smug look on his face. Everything in me wanted to tell him never mind and send him on his way. *"That's just your ego,"* my rational side said. *"You want honesty — now be honest yourself."*

"I have a real problem with anger," I repeated. "I know I overreact. It's all I've ever known. It's what my father did, but I don't want to be like that anymore," I said. His jaw was agape, and I could tell he never thought he would hear those words from me.

I began telling him everything I had realized while on the gurney. When I was done, I felt as if I had spent a few minutes in a confessional speeding through a lifetime of transgressions. He sat silently for a while and then took the offense.

"I want to get back together, but how can I be sure that this is for real?" he asked, sensing he now had the upper hand for the first time since the separation. I sat there for a moment, letting him bask in the feeling — but it was short-lived.

"I'm not the only one with problems," I said. "Don't get

me wrong, Doug. I told you I don't want a divorce. I don't, but if you keep lying, then I have no choice. I can't live with someone I can't trust." He looked deflated, and I could tell he was getting ready to launch a counterattack.

"You just said it wasn't all me, and now you are saying it is," he accused.

"No, that's not what I'm saying. I think the majority of our problems stem from the way I handle things, but at the same time, the problems themselves come from not being able to trust your word," I looked at him intensely. "We *both* have big problems that we *both* need to work on. I'm not willing to fall back into the same pattern we've had for seven years," I lectured. "I don't want us to just say we are going to do better, and then go right back to doing what we always do. We both have to be willing to really fix ourselves this time, or we don't have a chance. I don't want to live like that. Life is too short." There was that phrase again.

He stood up and started pacing the floor. I could tell his head was swimming too. I sat and waited patiently for him to digest the conversation.

"Okay," he finally mumbled, scratching his head. "I want this to work too, but we need to stay separated until we both are sure things have changed for good."

"I completely agree," I said.

"You have to prove to me you've changed," he added. Every hair on my body bristled, and I wanted to scream at him that he's the one who lied and cheated, but I swallowed it instead.

"I feel the same about you," I said calmly. "I need to know that you really want to change your need to lie, and I don't want you to do it for me. I want you to do it because it's what you want for yourself. Otherwise, it will never work."

I could see that I had taken him off his high horse, and I felt okay about it, because I had done it diplomatically instead of forcing it down his throat.

"I do want it for me," he sat down again and took my hands in his. We made plans to start seeing our counselor again immediately, and before it was all over with, I knew she would think she wasn't charging us enough.

Chapter Nine
The Lump

The next few weeks passed quickly. Softball was going well; Doug and I were seeing the counselor sometimes three times a week. We were making great strides in working out our problems.

Brea had just gotten out of school for the summer and was spending time with her friends. I was shuttling her back and forth for sleepovers.

One afternoon, I noticed that I had a lump on my wrist. At first, I thought it was my wrist bone, but then I noticed I already had a wrist bone. I was taking Brea to spend the night with her best friend Nikki. Nikki's parents, Ann and Bill, were good friends of ours, and Bill was an orthopedic surgeon. I walked Brea to the door and asked Ann if he was around, because I wanted to see what he thought about the lump.

"Sure, come on in," she said motioning me into her foyer. She left to get Bill. When he came back, I showed him my wrist.

"I found this on my wrist," I said showing him the knot. "I don't know how long it's been there. Do you know what it is?"

He turned my wrist over and felt the lump. "Does this hurt?" he asked.

"Nope," I said, "Not at all."

"Did you hit it on something?"

"No, not that I can remember."

"I don't really think it's anything, but if it doesn't get better, you can come in, and we'll x-ray it and get a better look."

I told him okay, said good-bye, and left.

The next day while getting Brea, I ran into Bill again.

"How's your hand?" he asked.

"Actually, I think it's gotten bigger," I said, looking at the bump.

He looked at my wrist. "Wow, it is bigger," he said, "just since yesterday. Does it hurt yet?"

"No, not really. It's kind of sore, but I think that's just because I've been rubbing it a lot this morning."

"I want you to call my office," he said. "I've got a great hand specialist. I think it's probably just a ganglion cyst, but we don't usually see them in this spot, and it's really too big. Anyway, let's let him look at it and see what he thinks."

I told him I would call the next morning. His nurse got

me in that afternoon, and I could tell Bill had told her not to make me wait. It was good to have friends in high places.

Bill came into the exam room first. "How's it doing today?" he asked picking up my hand.

"Still the same," I replied.

"My partner will be in here in a moment; he's just finishing up with someone."

We chitchatted until his partner arrived. Bill told him briefly about what he had seen, and then he mentioned that I had recently been diagnosed with breast cancer. His partner looked at me.

"How's everything going with that?" he asked.

"It's fine; I just had it removed. It was encased, so it wasn't really a big deal."

Bill left, and the specialist began examining my wrist. "I want to say this is just a ganglion cyst," he said, echoing Bill's initial thoughts. "But Bill's right, they are not usually located here, and they don't get that big. Let's get an MRI and figure it out," he said.

We were planning to leave for a family vacation to Mexico at the end of the week, and I told the doctor.

"No problem," he answered. "We can get you in tomorrow."

Overnight, I started getting concerned that the lump may not be just a cyst. I hadn't really given it much thought until Bill had made the point to tell his partner that I had cancer.

I looked at my wrist.

"*It's baaaack,*" the voice was like the one on *Poltergeist*, except that it belonged to Crazy Woman.

"*Oh God,*" I thought. I had actually not heard from her for a while, and I liked it that way.

"*It's baaaacck,*" she repeated.

"*Shut up. It's just a cyst,*" I told her.

"*Yeah right,*" she cackled as if I were the crazy one. "*What are the chances of a lump coming up on your wrist right after you had cancer?*" she chortled.

"*It can totally happen with no problem. Both of my doctors think it is just a cyst,*" I reasoned.

"*You know what this means, don't you?*"

I turned on the television to drown her out.

"*It means,*" she continued, "*that the cancer has spread, and now it's in your wrist. Actually, I bet it's everywhere.*"

"*That's not possible. It was confined to my ducts. They told me it hadn't gone anywhere...*"

She cut me off.

"*Like they know. They tell people that all the time, and then they die. Just like you are going to die.*"

I picked up the phone and called Doug.

"They want to do an MRI on my hand," I told him.

"Really? How come?" he asked.

"To see what the lump is."

"Okay," he paused, and I could tell he was wondering why I was acting weird. "When are you going to do it?" he finally said.

"In the morning. Do you think you could spend the night with me tonight?" I asked, wanting to keep Crazy Woman silent for the rest of the evening.

He could tell I was not in a good place.

"Sure, I'll be over after I work out," he said. "Maybe we can go get some dinner."

"That would be great," I said, and I sighed with relief. Anything I could do to keep busy and keep that psycho out of my head was welcome.

Chapter Ten
My Death

The next day I arrived at the MRI center.

As I lay in the massive machine, I thought about our upcoming trip. I badly needed to get away, and I was glad it was about to happen. Halfway through the procedure, the door to the control room opened, and the technician came to the side of the machine.

"I'm sorry, Ms. Shelton, but we are going to have to take some extra pictures. Something doesn't look right."

I stopped breathing. "What do you mean?" I asked.

"Well, the radiologist says there's something strange about the mass. He wants to get a few extra scans. It will probably take another half hour. I know it's difficult lying in this position, but just stay still a little longer, and we'll get you out of here as soon as possible."

I felt every anxiety I had been suppressing begin welling

up inside me. It started in my stomach and slowly began creeping up my throat.

"*Stop it. Don't you dare cry,*" I told myself. "*These people will think you are insane, crying over a bump on your wrist. Don't you dare cry.*"

My scolding didn't work. Water began leaking from my eyes. Shortly after, my nose was running. I had no tissue, and I had been told to lie perfectly still. The water and snot dripped down my face. "*You are going to die,*" Crazy Woman taunted. "*I told you so. This is it. The cancer is everywhere, and you will not be here a year from now.*"

"*Stop it, stop it, stop it,*" I told her. "*This is nothing. Everything is going to be okay,*" I tried convincing her and myself. "*I am going to live to be a hundred. Brealyn will not have to be without me,*" I challenged her.

The thought of leaving my daughter caused me to start shaking. I was not afraid to die, but I was terrified at the thought of leaving Brea alone in the world to fend for herself. It was my worst possible nightmare, and I could not even begin to wrap my mind around it.

After what seemed like years, the technician came back into the room. My shirt was soaked, and there was a small puddle of tears and mucus on the bed of the machine. As the bed moved out of the tunnel, I tried to wipe my face so that the tech would not see I had been crying. I kept my head down, hiding my red and swollen face, and I turned away from him as much as I could while he explained what would come next.

I didn't grasp any of it, because my mind was racing too fast. I knew I had to get out of that room as soon as I could, because the dam was about to break.

As soon as I got in my car, my body heaved into sobs. I couldn't think, I couldn't drive, I couldn't function.

"*Calm down. You have to calm down. This is not helping anything!*" I tried reasoning with myself.

"*Brealyn is not going to survive this,*" Crazy Woman answered.

"*Breathe, you have to breathe. Yes, I've got to breathe,*" I answered, and I did.

I knew I had to calm down enough to drive home, but at the same time, I knew I couldn't go home. If I did, Crazy Woman would put me over the edge. I decided I needed help.

I picked up my cell phone and called our counselor, Elaine. She was by far the best counselor we had seen and had been more helpful in one session than the previous three had been in five years.

My shaking hands dialed her number.

"Elaine, I've got to see you now," I said, crying. She agreed, and I drove to her office.

"Sit down," she said when she opened the door. She motioned me to a small couch. She could tell I was a wreck.

I sat there crying for a moment and then blew my nose. I told her what had happened and then blurted out, "I'm not afraid of dying, but Brealyn won't survive this."

She cocked her head to one side, looking perplexed. Her

brow furrowed, and she leaned into me so she could look directly in my face.

"Stacy, that's just not true," she said calmly, shaking her head.

I was shocked. She obviously didn't understand the connection that Brea and I had.

"You don't understand," I protested. "It has been just the two of us for most of her life. We are closer than any mother and daughter I know," I tried convincing her. "You know how people say that their spouses are their soul mates? Well, I've never thought that, because Brealyn is my soul mate." I stopped to wipe my tears.

"From the moment the child came into this world, I've known she was my purpose," I rambled, "and I am hers. If I die, she will not be able to make it." I pleaded my case, trying to get her to understand our connection.

"Stacy," she said calmly, "you are wrong. I don't doubt that she is your reason for existing, but you are not hers."

She might as well have slapped me.

"Let's walk through this rationally," she continued. "I think it will really help for you to get some perspective on this."

She let me wipe my eyes and nose again, and then she sat back in her chair. "Let's say worst case scenario — you die," she looked at me, trying to gage my response.

I was shaking my head no; so she paused, waiting for me to process the idea.

"I know this is hard," she said, "but stay with me. I think I can help you."

I nodded yes, letting her know I had regained enough composure to continue.

"If you are gone," she said gently, "do you have a way to take care of her financially?"

I thought about it for a moment.

"Yes," I sniffed. "I have a life insurance policy that goes to her. It will at least get her through college, and then some," I reluctantly answered.

"Okay good. Let's look at where she will live. Do you have family that you want to leave her with?"

"She would live with her dad," I answered, still wary of the fact that I wouldn't be around to watch and try to control her every move.

"Is that a good thing or a bad thing?" Elaine questioned.

"It's good, I guess. She loves her dad. They talk two or three times a day. They are very close."

"Excellent. Does he live here?" she questioned.

"No."

"So that means she will have to move?"

"Yes," I said, starting to cry again. I didn't want her to be uprooted.

"Wait a minute," she scolded. "I know you think that's bad, but is it really?"

"What do you mean?"

"Is Brea a wallflower, or is she the kind of kid that makes friends easily?"

"She's a social butterfly." I began to giggle through my snot.

"See," she soothed, "it's not such a bad thing. What other kind of support system does she have?" she continued.

"She's got an aunt and uncle that live there too, and she's got friends that she knew before we moved."

"Okay then, Stacy, do you see that everything will work out for her? Sure, she will miss you. She will cry, and she may even get depressed because she misses you, but she will survive without you. Kids are resilient, and they can make it through the loss of a parent and a whole lot worse."

As much as I didn't want to admit my daughter would make it without me, it was evident that she would.

I felt my blood pressure drop, and the weight of the world that I had been carrying on my shoulders lightened. I closed my eyes, envisioning this planet without me on it. It was still beautiful, and it was still spinning. My daughter walked among her peers, her family, and ultimately, her own children. She was smiling and content. She was okay, and so was I.

It would take me some time to realize it, but walking myself through my own death had been one of the most liberating things I had ever done. In fact, it was a gift.

It allowed me to begin living my life authentically for the first time ever. I never again wanted to allow myself to make decisions based on fear. And I didn't know it then, but I was about to have to make some of the most monumental decisions of my life.

Two days passed before I heard from the specialist. "We

are almost positive it's just a ganglion cyst." I breathed a sigh of relief at his words. "It's going to require surgery," he added, "but we can take care of it when you get back from vacation."

"Thank you so much," I whispered. "Thank you."

When we got home, with Doug by my side this time, I had the surgery, and all went well.

Chapter Eleven
Life Is Too Short

The rest of the summer was passing quickly. In July, we got word that a cousin, who was like a brother to Doug, had died in a motorcycle accident. He left behind five children. Doug was devastated.

We made the nine-hour trip to Iowa for the funeral. Doug was withdrawn for the majority of it. I knew he wanted to talk about his feelings, but I also knew he couldn't find the words.

During the funeral, he sat stoically, showing no emotion. But when we went to the cemetery and they lowered his cousin into the ground, he lost it. He walked off by himself, and I followed. I had never seen him cry like that before, and I was at a loss for how to help him. I pulled him to me and laid his head on my shoulder. He sobbed.

That night in the motel room, we lay awake talking.

"He was so young." Doug shook his head. "Life is so fragile, so short."

There it was again, staring us in the face — life is too short. It seemed as if we were being reminded of that at every turn, and I began wondering if we would ever be able to go back to that place where we could be oblivious to that fact.

Doug turned on his side and looked into my eyes.

"I love you," he said, "and I don't want to lose you."

"I don't want to lose you either," I paused. "I know it hasn't been very long since we started working with Elaine, but I think we've come farther than I ever expected," I acknowledged.

"I agree," he said.

We lay in silence for a few more moments, weighing the events that had brought us to that moment.

"Are you ready to get back together?" I asked, turning my head to look at him.

"Yes," he replied.

And we did.

The fall came, Brea and I moved back home, immersing ourselves in our former lives. I could tell from the moment we got back that we had made the right decision. We were still seeing Elaine but not as frequently. Each session, it seemed as if we had less and less to work out until she finally said. "If you need me, I'm here, but I think you guys can handle it yourselves."

We got caught up in being in love. We would walk, holding hands, to the football games at the local university, wake up together snuggling, and have coffee on our patio, enjoying being side by side again. Life was as good as it had ever been for me, and best of all, Crazy Woman was gone.

The author and her family: Brealyn, Douglas and Oliver

Chapter Twelve
It's Back

In October, about four weeks before I was scheduled to have my six-month follow-up mammogram, I began having a sharp stinging pain in my right breast — the same breast where I previously had cancer.

At first, I told myself it was probably just scar tissue growing and making me uncomfortable. But day after day, it continued to get worse. Finally, I told Doug that I thought I would move my appointment up to ease my mind. "It won't be anything," I said, fully believing it, "but at least maybe she can tell me what's going on and give me something for the pain."

I called the next day, but the nurse told me I would have to wait another two weeks for an opening. It meant that I was only moving up my appointment by one week.

I sat in the nicely furnished waiting room with at least a dozen other women and some husbands who had been forced to accompany their wives.

"*I will be so glad to get this over with,*" I told myself. "*A clean mammogram and I'm good to go.*"

"*What if it's not clean?*" Crazy Woman announced her return.

"*Oh God, not you,*" I sighed, gritting my teeth. "*You will not wreak havoc on me again,*" I warned. "*There is no way I have it. I am perfectly healthy.*"

"Ms. Shelton," I heard a nurse say from the doorway. It was my cue to follow her. She led me to a little closet with a gray locker.

"Put on this gown. It closes in front." She handed me a mauve smock. "And then take a seat right there," she said, pointing to a smaller waiting room across the hall. "The tech will be here in just a moment to get you." She closed the door and left me to get topless.

I walked to the waiting room and sat in the closest chair. Another woman sat to my left and I said a halfhearted, "Hello," while picking out a magazine. I tried pretending to read it, but Crazy Woman kept butting in.

"*What if...*"

"Stop it," I muttered under my breath. "*Everything is going to be great. I am perfectly healthy,*" I silently repeated.

"Okay, Ms. Shelton?" A large woman in pink scrubs asked as she stuck her head in the doorway.

"That's me," I answered, rising to follow her.

She took me to the same room I had been in six months earlier, leading me through the same process as before.

After the procedure, the nurse told me to stay in the smock and return to the small waiting room.

"We just want to make sure the films are all okay before we let you get dressed," the portly woman said. It was all eerily déjà vu.

I went back to the same chair I had just left, and once again picked up the magazine. The room was empty, and I heard myself let out a long and loud sigh.

Waiting was awkward. I felt like a child who had committed some egregious offense and had been sent to the principal's office. I couldn't shake the feeling of trouble, but I kept talking myself down.

The minutes passed and I became antsy. Random thoughts invaded my mind, like tiny explosions of fireworks. Each time one would pop, I would stop it, not giving it room to spread. When I knew it had been too long for the news to be good, the nurse appeared in the doorway.

"Ms. Shelton, we are going to need to take a couple of more pictures."

In a split-second, I became one of those transformers that changes from a car into a robot, only I changed from someone respectful to someone who more resembled Crazy Woman. "Why?" I tersely demanded.

"We didn't get what we needed the first time," she answered as she tried to avoid looking at me. I took her avoidance as a dare and glared at her without saying anything, until she had to return my gaze.

"What do you mean you didn't get the pictures you need-ed? You took twenty pictures," I exaggerated. "You're tell-ing me you didn't take enough to get the right ones?" My voice became an octave higher.

"Well," she tried explaining, "the radiologist wants to see further up under your arm. We didn't get far enough."

I was instantly mad and I was about to cry.

I knew the anger was irrational, and I understood that I wasn't really mad — I was scared. I had already been there and done that, and I knew, without her saying it, that they had found something. I reluctantly stood and followed her back into the boob dungeon from hell.

After the second set of pictures, the nurse told me to wait inside the room. I sat in a small plastic chair, mindlessly staring at the wall. In less than five minutes, the radiologist appeared. I looked at him, waiting for him tell me what I already knew.

"It appears that there are more calcifications in your breast," he sighed. "Almost in the same place as before."

I was numb and didn't respond.

"You're left breast looks good," though, he added, obvi-ously thinking that would make me feel better.

I looked down at the floor. "*Show no emotion. Put your big girl panties on and don't let him see that you are really just one nanosecond away from screaming,*" I told myself.

"I'm going to send these to your surgeon right now," he

continued. "I don't think we should wait. Is that okay with you?" he asked.

I nodded my head and took a deep breath, knowing that I needed to regain my composure enough to ask him questions before he left.

"Are there a lot of them?" I asked.

"It appears there may be more than before."

"Can you tell if they have spread?" I could feel myself getting back into control.

"They are still encased in the ducts, which is good news," he answered. "The important thing is to see your surgeon as soon as possible. I'm not really supposed to be talking to you about it. That's her job," he was almost apologizing.

By this time, I had completely recovered and had on my game face. I stood up and shook his hand.

"I appreciate the information," I told him. "I'll call right away."

He left the room at the same time the nurse entered. "You're free to get dressed now," she said. I nodded and went to the dressing room, my head spinning.

I can't help but reflect on the fact that both times I was diagnosed, my gut knew in advance. I didn't want to believe it, but I knew it.

The first time, the pink ribbon symbol of breast cancer kept showing up in my life in the weirdest ways. Since the passing of both of my grandmothers, signs have appeared to give me guidance. I believe these signs come from my grandmothers whom I think of as my angels. I can't explain it, but I have come to rely on them every bit as much as I rely on the daily weather report.

The Native American people believe that there are signs everywhere to help us on our journey. I had studied this several years earlier and came to believe that there is great truth to it.

About six months before my first diagnosis, the pink ribbon began showing up. Because of my belief that "thoughts are things," I refused to acknowledge that there might be a problem. Every time I saw the sign, I would say in my head, or aloud if I was alone, "*I do not have breast cancer. I am healthy.*" However, there would always be a nagging doubt and then another sign.

One of them happened about six weeks before I finally scheduled the first mammogram. Because of my hip replacements, I need to wear a specific type of running shoe, which has a roll bar to keep my foot steady. It also helped with pain that I experienced in my thighs.

I'd been looking for the shoe over six months, unable to find it. Finally, I found a store that could order it for me. When I got the shoe and tried it on, there on the tongue was the pink ribbon. It had to have been the hundredth pink ribbon I had seen in a matter of weeks. I knew I couldn't ignore it anymore. "Someone" was trying to tell me something, and I reluctantly made the appointment.

This time, the warning came in the form of the pain I was having. When I felt it, my first thought was that the pain was a sign that it was back. I clearly remember "feeling" as if I should have it checked, but I refused to go there, again telling myself that I was perfectly healthy. After several weeks of it though, the feeling got stronger and I gave in. The fact that it was a sign was confirmed when as soon as I was diagnosed that day, I never had the pain again.

Chapter Thirteen
Lost

On the drive home from the mammography center, my head was filled with a numbing, buzzing noise. I pulled into my garage and walked into our family room. I slid onto the couch, letting numbness overtake my body.

"I need to tell Doug," I thought.

"If you tell him, he is going to resent you." Crazy Woman appeared again. I shook my head no. She snickered.

"He will pretend to be supportive. He will tell you he will be right there with you, but in reality, the minute you go bald, he is going to resent you. He'll think, 'Oh crap, I'm married to a bald woman.' And the next time he's with all his friends and they are talking about their sexy wives, he'll be pitied unmercifully."

"What are you talking about?" I screamed at her, tears streaming down my face.

"You *know exactly what I'm talking about. They'll be talking about their wives, and they'll look at Doug and think, 'Poor sap, he's having sex with a boob-less cue ball.'*"

"*Shut up,*" I pleaded. "*Just shut up.*"

I sat there wiping my face and nose with my sleeve, telling myself to pick up the phone and call him.

"*Calm down first,*" I reasoned, not wanting to be one of those hysterical women who starts sobbing uncontrollably the second she hears her husband's voice.

I sank back onto the couch and looked over at my saltwater aquarium. I had the aquarium for over a year and had fallen in love with it. I would sit for hours watching all the marine life and forgetting about mine. I climbed into the chair beside it, sat on my knees, nose pressed against the warm glass. My Valentina Puffer swam to me and smiled.

"Hey, Val," I said to the little black and white-striped fish with the yellow tale. "I have breast cancer." Val looked at me, little fish lips pursed, and fanned his tail. Then he swam away.

Chub Chub, the starfish, was slowly moving across the bottom of the tank, completely oblivious to my news. I tried to sit and stay focused, but I couldn't keep still. It was as if there were a thousand needles pricking my legs. I felt like I could fire lightning bolts from my fingertips. It was soon obvious that my fish would not be able to comfort me that day.

I slid back down into the chair and relived the previous hour of my life.

"*Call your husband,*" my brain said again. "*He can calm you down. He will be able to help.*"

Hesitantly, I picked up the phone and dialed the number. As his receptionist answered the phone, I felt myself starting to choke up, so I coughed to disguise the cracking in my voice.

"Hi, can I speak with Doug?"

She put me on hold and the tears began welling.

"*Calm yourself down, you big baby,*" I heard Crazy Woman scold. "*You need to get a grip. You can't fall apart because someone has told you that you have...*"

"Hey, baby," my husband said. He always sounded so glad to talk to me when I called. This time, it made me want to cry even more.

"I need to tell you something," I said.

"Okay, what's up?" he asked curiously.

"I have breast cancer again."

Silence.

Dead Silence.

"What do you mean?" he finally asked, afraid to hear the answer, but before I could, he continued. "Again? Are you sure? In the same breast? In the other breast? How do you know? I mean what..." I cut him off.

"I went back today because of the pain I was having, and they said I have exactly what I had before. Only this time, there is more of it."

"In the other breast?" he asked.

"No, same one," I said, not believing it. "The radiologist

sent the films to my surgeon already. He says I need to get in to see her as soon as possible."

I went back to that moment in my head and let the line go silent, remembering the news. I heard my husband clear his throat, and I snapped back to the present.

"Okay then, that's what we have to do," he said in his best "I am totally in control, never let them see you sweat" lawyer voice. "We will get it biopsied, and I bet it will be nothing."

We both sat quietly for a moment, then he cleared his throat again.

"And, baby, no matter what, I'm with you on this."

Then I cried.

"I know," I managed while trying to stifle sobs. "I know."

Chapter Fourteen
Telling Again

Sometimes, I have a dream that my teeth are breaking off or falling out. In my dream, my mouth is full of broken teeth, and I scoop them out; but then there are more, so I just keep scooping and pushing all these little pieces of teeth out with my tongue. I wonder how there can be so much stuff to keep scooping out of my mouth, and I am mortified that I am losing my teeth.

I start thinking of all the ways I should have taken better care of them, like flossing more and brushing longer, and I am so embarrassed because I am toothless.

In these dreams, I immediately try to find my brother, who is a dentist. When I do, he takes one look at my teeth and just starts shaking his head.

The dream is a common one that means the person having it feels as if they've lost control of their life or that they may be afraid of aging or even dying. That obviously fit me to a tee. The way I felt in those dreams — scared, embarrassed, helpless, and hopeless — was exactly the way I felt then. My life was just as mixed-up, crazy, upside down, backwards, and strange as it was when I dreamed. The only difference was I could not wake up.

I again sat down by the aquarium, trying to get myself under control. I thought about how I was going to have to tell my family and friends — for a second time — that I had cancer. The thoughts scattered like light rays. *"They are not going to believe this. They are going to treat you differently. What am I supposed to say to them?"* Then the big one hit — my daughter — I had to tell Brealyn again, and I knew this time she was not going to be as calm.

I looked at the clock. I had less than an hour before I would pick her up from school. I began forming my game plan, which was very similar to the first one. I decided not to tell her until I could pull myself together and act like it was no big deal. For all she would know, nothing had changed. I would be the same, pain-in-the-butt, intruding mother that she knew and loved. I immediately felt better.

I sat in silence staring at the blank screen of the television. I could see my reflection in it. I lifted a piece of my long blond hair wondering what I would look like bald. I was always vain about my looks, and although I had put on some weight since my hip replacements, I still thought I looked pretty good for my forty-one years.

"I'm not telling anyone," I said aloud to the blond in the TV. "Not yet." Then I curled up into a ball and closed my eyes. A tear slipped down my cheek as my mind replayed the memories of the little girl I had birthed fifteen years before. Her giggles and frowns forever etched into my brain.

"*I cannot leave her,*" echoed like a recorded loop in my brain. "*She needs me.*"

That night, as soon as I could find a minute alone, I searched the Internet for treatment centers in our area. I was uncomfortable going back in and just having the cancer removed as I had before. It was no longer okay with just taking the first option given. I wanted other options, and I wanted to know that I was getting the absolute, state-of the-art treatment for people with recurring cancer.

I found a hospital nearby that specialized in breast cancer. It was the same hospital that Laura had suggested before. They had a doctor that was doing a nationwide study on a new form of radioactive seed treatment. As luck would have it, I had been introduced to the man who invented the radioactive seed treatment for prostate cancer. I knew it had a great track record.

The next day, I called to make an appointment with my previous surgeon as well as the one I had found the night before. The second hospital informed me that the doctor conducting the research was no longer taking patients, but they had another surgeon who was also involved and had a great reputation. I made an appointment with her for the day following my first appointment.

That evening, Doug made it very clear that he was going with me to all my appointments.

"I know you don't need me there, but I want to be. I don't feel like I know what's going on after the last time, and I have a lot of questions too. I hope you're okay with that."

I was more than okay with it. I needed his strength and someone who could focus.

In the following days, I tried to figure out a way to tell my friends and family. I realized there was no "way"; I just had to do it. I picked up the phone and dialed, calling Laura first. I heard a loud sigh on the other end.

"Oh no," she said, and I heard all the energy drain from her body. "It's okay," she recovered and put on her "We're going to kick some butt" game face. "You can handle this, and it's going to be okay." I nodded in agreement. She was someone that I completely trusted, because she always called it like she saw it. If she said I was going to be okay, then you could bet money on it.

I found myself consoling everyone else, most of whom were devastated.

"It's going to be fine. We are going to see two surgeons and get options from them both. I'll call you after we talk to them," I said to my friends Kathy, Pam, Karin, Barbara and Ann.

Then I continued through my list, telling everyone the same thing. The only thing left to do was tell Brealyn, and I dreaded that more than anything.

I wish I could say I remember the conversation with her, but I don't. I have no memory of it at all. Undergoing anesthesia causes me to lose some of my memory. Because I had seven surgeries in twenty-seven months, large parts of my memory of that time are gone. Our conversation was one of the things that left, never to return.

I can only speculate that it went okay because during all of my recovery time I only remember her having one minor breakdown. One evening, she was being testy and I was chastising her for acting out. She burst into tears saying she was just "stressed out."

"Why are you stressed, Brealyn?" I queried, wondering how the life of a fifteen-year-old could cause that much discomfort.

She reminded me that during the past year, she had lost her grandmother and an uncle on her father's side. She explained that her stress was due to that and my getting cancer.

I consoled her, telling her that everything was going to be fine. "I know you lost Memaw and Uncle Larry," I said. "but you aren't getting rid of me. I'm going to be around a long time to ride your butt to make sure you are making As and cleaning your room." She giggled and hugged me, and that was the end of that.

One of the author's biggest support groups, her friends: Pam Hooper, Laura Ingram, the author, Kathy McIver and Jenny Ladner.

Chapter Fifteen
A Different Avenue

Doug and I met with my original surgeon. We both asked questions about the return of the cancer.

"Is this normal? Do people get it again this soon?"

"Not usually" was the answer.

"Is this left over, or is it new?"

She told us she believed it was new, because I had clean margins after the first surgery. We also talked about how to proceed.

"Your options are a little different now, since we aren't dealing with a first-time occurrence," she said. She explained that until the tissue was biopsied, we wouldn't know exactly how to proceed.

I don't know how Doug felt when we left, but I was confused. My brain wasn't working as it should. There was so much swimming around in it that I couldn't compartmentalize it. It was just a hodgepodge bunch of mush bombarding my every thought.

I had to ask Doug repeatedly what had been said and how the doctor answered. It was as if my brain was completely filled to the brim, rendering it useless to process new information.

The following day, we saw the new surgeon. When she walked into the room, she had a calm and soothing demeanor, making me instantly comfortable.

Because we had never met her, our questions were more extensive, and I wanted to know her philosophy for treating the disease. She quoted the latest studies on ductal carcinoma insitu. She knew statistics that supported her concerns. It became obvious that breast cancer was her specialty.

She was also not afraid to get blunt with me, and that's a trait that my overbearing personality appreciated. I'm a black and white thinker about most things. She gave us facts and statistics for my chances of reoccurrence and for my cure. We did not ask one question that she couldn't answer.

She was also remarkably kind and sensitive, allowing some of my anxiety to melt. She acted as if she had all the time in the world when I knew her waiting room said otherwise.

The more we spoke, the more I became convinced that she should be my doctor. My thoughts were confirmed when she looked over my file from the previous surgery.

"I'm not sure why they told you that you had clean margins," she said with a puzzled look on her face.

"What do you mean?" Doug and I both asked.

"Well, this shows that the size of the area biopsied wasn't really that large. We don't claim that the margins are clear unless we have several centimeters of tissue outside the area of cancer that is clean. Yes, the margins of the tissue that was taken were clear, but I don't think there was enough tissue actually taken," she added.

Doug and I looked at each other.

"So you're saying that I may have had this before, and they just didn't get it?"

"I don't really think so," she said. "If it was there, the mammogram should have shown it when they looked at the tissue again after the surgery. My guess is that they got it all the first time. I just would have liked to have seen more tissue in the biopsy."

That information brought a completely different dimension to the equation. Although she was confident that I was having a reoccurrence instead of residual cancer, I was uncomfortable not knowing for sure. However, it didn't matter. The fact was, it was there; and I needed to handle it, whatever the case.

We exhausted our questions, and I asked the doctor if I could talk to Doug alone. She obliged, telling us to take our time as she left to see another patient.

"I want her to be my surgeon," I said when she left. "She has a lot of expertise. I already know more in the twenty minutes we've been with her than I learned in the past six months."

"Are you sure?" he asked. "I'm not telling you I don't

agree; I just want to make sure you are comfortable. You don't have to make a decision today. We have time. The most important thing is that you are comfortable."

"I'm positive," I replied. "She's the one — I feel it."

The doctor gently knocked on the door. "May I come in?" she asked.

She entered the room and I told her of my decision.

"Okay," she said, "Let's talk about a treatment plan."

I could feel my stomach tightening. I knew this plan was not going to be the cakewalk I had previously.

"First, we need to remove the cancer," she said. "I don't think we need to biopsy because of your history. It just needs to come out. Then we can decide after we see pathology reports how we should proceed from there. Is that okay with you?"

My brain was still swimming, and I welcomed the time between the surgery and the pathology report to process the new information we had been given.

"Yes, I think that's what we should do," I said, exhaling.

"Then let's schedule the surgery for next week. I'll have you both come back for a follow-up a week post-op, and we'll go over the reports. We can make a game plan then," she said, getting up to leave. We shook her hand and thanked her for her time.

Walking out of her office, we knew we were about to turn the page to a new chapter in our lives, one that neither of us was prepared to enter.

Chapter Sixteen
Fuzzy White Socks

For the next week, I walked around with a constant gnawing in my brain. It wasn't Crazy Woman, but it was a small hissing voice that echoed, bouncing off every side of my skull.

"You have cancer in your body. You have cancer in your body. You have cancer in your body." It was constant and relentless, and thinking clearly about anything else was next to impossible.

With every breath I took, I was only a nanosecond away from a total meltdown. My skin crawled. I could not get comfortable inside my own body. Every thought was like an electrical circuit misfiring. Each place I sat was uncomfortable. Every conversation I had felt as if I were trying to speak while underwater. Each night's sleep was interrupted second after second with crazy, rolling, nonsensical dreams.

Nothing, no one, and no place could give me the peace for which my soul was screaming.

Finally, one night after putting on my pajamas in preparation for another sleepless night, my feet became chilled. I went to my closet and pulled out a pair of fuzzy, white house socks. They were the type of socks that are so thick you can't squeeze your foot into a pair of shoes, and they were as soft and cozy as a cloud. When I slipped them on my feet, I felt a sense of peace come over me that I had not known in weeks. I felt normal.

Looking back, it had been the most normal thing I had done since my diagnosis. I had done it without thinking. Somehow, the socks comforted me, and I actually heard myself breathe a sigh of relief. It was as if they transported me to a place where I was guaranteed that everything would be okay. Those socks became my escape, and if I was home, they were on my feet.

I spent the rest of the days before my surgery going through the motions of life.

One night, while making love with my husband, I lay silently trying to keep my thoughts at bay. It didn't work.

"Psst, it's me, Cancer. Just wanted you to know I'm still here."

"Yes, I'm painfully aware of that," I silently acknowledged.

"Good, I just wanted to make sure you knew where I was coming from."

"Where are you coming from?" I asked, wondering if it had some important life lesson for me — a great enlightenment.

"Your boob."

I rolled my eyes. Obviously it was a student of Crazy Woman.

I snapped out of it. It was clear my mental state was a huge mess. I was having an imaginary conversation with the stupid cancer instead of concentrating on the time with Doug.

"God," I thought, *"if he had any idea what was going on in my head right now."*

But he didn't. He was happy as a clam.

Chapter Seventeen
Unraveling

We arose early the day of the surgery, and Doug drove me to the hospital. Again, the nurses explained how they would thread a long wire through my breast after compressing it, making sure to surround the cancer. My nerves were completely on edge, and I was irritated beyond reason. It was clear that Crazy Woman was about to make an appearance.

"Shelton!" a heavy-set nurse yelled from the doorway.

Doug let go of my hand as I stood to meet her. "Can my husband come?" I asked her.

"No, hon," she drawled. "It's better that he stay here."

That was not what I wanted to hear.

I felt like I had consumed a hundred cups of coffee — my mind buzzing and, again, my skin crawling. I needed Doug to be with me because of the horror that awaited me. My eyes started to tear — an angry tearing. I didn't know how I was going to make the walk to the mammography room without him. I let Crazy Woman take over.

"Why can't he come?" she challenged.

"Well, the room is really not big enough for all of us," she answered. To which Crazy Woman silently replied, *"Because of your fat ass."*

I looked back at Doug like a puppy who was about to be put down. He assured me he would be there waiting when I was done.

She led me to the room, which was easily large enough for all of us, and told me to put on a flowered smock.

"We're going to need to take some pictures of your breast first," she said.

Crazy Woman was having none of that.

"No," she answered. "You already have the ones from the mammography center. They show where the cancer is. You can use those," she demanded.

"We really can't do that." The nurse looked alarmed.

"Well, you are going to have to," Crazy Woman said. "Because there is no reason to do it again, especially when you already have what you need," she bullied, daring the woman to take her on again.

"Just a minute," the nurse replied, backing away from the obviously insane person in front of her. "Let me ask my supervisor if we can use these."

"You go ahead, but I'm telling you, until you are putting the wire in, there will be no more pictures," Crazy Woman informed.

I sat in the very cold room praying that the nurse would not come through the door with any answer other than the one I wanted. At the same time, I could feel myself unraveling like a steel cable asked to carry too much weight.

She came back. "Okay," she said reluctantly, "we can use the films you brought."

"I told you," Crazy Woman retorted. She obviously took this as a sign that she was now in control. "And turn up the thermostat," she commanded. "It's ridiculously cold in here."

The nurse became tense, sensing that she was about to have another sparring round.

"I can't do that," she hesitated. "It has to be cool in here for the machines to operate correctly," she reasoned.

Crazy Woman was about to unleash and tell the woman that she knew that was a sack of crap and that the only reason it was so cold was so her obese butt wouldn't sweat, but I regained control and overtook her.

"Okay," I answered.

I sat shivering as she compressed my breast in the mammography machine. I continued to shiver and shake as she threaded the long wire through my tissue and around the cancer. I held every breath I could until she was done. Then she led me back to the waiting room and my husband.

He looked up from his newspaper and gasped. I was white as a sheet.

"Are you okay?" he asked, alarmed. I grabbed his hand and led him out of the room and into a hall. I collapsed on a bench and began sobbing, the wire hanging loosely from my side. I incoherently tried to explain what I had just gone through and how incredibly mad I was at the stupid nurse who wouldn't turn up the heat. He stroked my hair while telling me it was okay.

I can only imagine how insane I must have seemed to him at that moment because, well, I was. At the same time, I knew I wasn't really angry at the nurse. I was just angry. I was more than angry. I was enraged, incensed, and irate that I had this cruel disease again and there was nothing I could do about it. I was, for the first time in my life, fully aware that I had absolutely no control over my own life. I had never been more scared.

Chapter Eighteen
Choices

The surgery went much the same as the last one had, except this time, my husband was by my side. I lost consciousness only to be awakened by the surgeon.

"Everything went great, Stacy," she said, arousing me from the nothingness. I heard bits and pieces about taking larger amounts of tissue, something about pathology reports and seeing her again in a few days, but I decided that Doug could handle the details. I drifted back into unconsciousness.

The following week, Doug and I returned to the surgeon's office for my post-surgical follow-up.

"It was cancer," the surgeon said as she entered the room. We both sat, stoic. There had never been any question in our minds.

"The pathology said it was more aggressive this time,"

she continued. I raised my eyebrows.

"Does that mean invasive?" I asked.

"No, it was still DCIS — still contained in the ducts — but it had more receptors, and it was growing faster," she explained. "What we have to do now is discuss your options." She looked at us both and waited for a response.

Crazy Woman was yelling *"Chemo!"* in my head but outwardly, we were both silent.

"Okay," she continued. "Here are your options. We can start you on radiation treatments right away…" I interrupted her.

"I chose this hospital because it offered the radioactive seed. I think I would rather do that than the traditional form," I stated.

She looked at my chart a moment. "I think you would be a good candidate for it," she said, nodding her head. "We can also begin a regimen of tamoxifen."

I winced. I don't know why I carried such an aversion to the medication other than my belief that less is more when it comes to drugs. I tend to think if it's not naturally occurring in your body or on the planet, then I don't want it in my body.

If she noticed my wincing, she didn't show it. "Now," she said, taking a seat, "there is another option, considering this is a reoccurrence and considering you have a family history."

Again, Crazy Woman yelled, *"Chemo!"*

What came next was even worse than the chemo Crazy

Woman had been using to taunt me.

"You might want to consider a mastectomy."

Time stopped.

The mere idea of chopping off the body parts that most defined who I was as a woman was too big of a concept to grasp. My mind refused — with a capital "R" — to go there. I stopped breathing as if the act could stop the moment from happening.

"No!" I half yelled, half whispered. "That's just not an option for me." I looked at Doug, my eyes begging him to back me up.

She saw my shock and quickly retreated.

"Well, remember, It's not your only option," she soothed. "We have had a lot of success with just the partial mastectomy and radiation."

I exhaled, knowing I had to acknowledge Crazy Woman's concern.

"What about chemo?" I asked, deflated.

"No, you won't have to have chemotherapy. The cancer was contained to the ducts," she reiterated.

"*So there,*" I silently told Crazy Woman. "*Just shut up for once.*"

"Okay, radiation then," I murmured, again looking at Doug. Radiation I could handle. "*No worse than a sunburn,*" I told myself, relaxing.

"But," came the words I dreaded, "I have a suggestion that I want you to think about. We have a test that will tell us if you carry the genes for breast cancer."

She explained that because this was my second go-round and because I had a family history, I should consider it. "It may help you make a more informed decision," she said.

"What do you mean 'more informed decision'?" I asked, already knowing in the back of my mind she thought I had made the wrong one about the radiation.

"If you carry the gene," she explained, "you have an eighty-percent chance in your lifetime of the cancer reoccurring. The next time, it could very well be invasive. Then, it's a whole new ballgame," she paused, taking a breath. "If you carry the gene, you really have no option. You have to get the mastectomies, because if you don't, you are playing a game where the odds are very heavily stacked against you."

I envisioned playing Russian roulette with every chamber but one having a bullet in it instead of every chamber empty except one.

"*Why are you doing this?*" I wanted to scream. "*I thought you understood that a mastectomy is not an option!*"

My head was swimming in the sewage she just unleashed on me.

"*Calm down and get some more information,*" my sane self was saying. I listened to that part.

"Okay, tell me about the test," I answered meekly.

Doug was beginning to get pale.

"It's a really easy blood test," she continued, explaining that my insurance may not cover it.

"They might, because it's a reoccurrence. If they don't, it will cost around three thousand dollars. But at any rate, at least we would know what we are dealing with. The problem is it takes about four weeks to get the results."

The weight of the world became a whole lot heavier. Not only had I learned that I might have to cut off my breasts, now she wanted me to live in limbo another four weeks before making the decision.

I couldn't imagine sitting around another day stewing in this cesspool, much less a month. My life had been consumed with the shock that the cancer was back again — my body betraying me in the worst possible way. Realizing I wasn't even close to having my life or my mind back was almost more than I could take.

"Are you kidding me?" I asked incredulously. "Four weeks? I'm just supposed to sit here for another four weeks and wait? What if the cancer comes back?"

"I'm sorry," she tried to soothe me. "It's a DNA test, so it takes a long time. I believe it's a helpful tool that we need in this case, but the decision is yours."

Sensing that I needed a voice of reason, Doug took my hand. "Honey, I think it's a good idea. We need to know. If you don't carry the gene, then we can just do the radiation. I bet you won't carry it," he said, squeezing my hand and giving me a glimmer of hope.

I backed down. "Okay."

"It will be good for your daughter too," she added. "If you carry the gene, she is going to have to take extra precautions with her health."

I wanted to throw up. I hadn't even thought about Brea.

How do you tell a fifteen-year-old child that she may be destined for cancer? "Guess what I got for you today, honey? Cancer!"

The surgeon saw my terror. "I know this is difficult, but knowledge is power. If you carry it, then we can be diligent with her health. We will have the upper hand."

I reluctantly nodded my dizzy head.

"I'll make the arrangements," she said. "We'll be in touch." She shook both of our hands and left.

I looked at Doug. "Here we go again," I sighed.

"It's okay," he answered. "We can handle this. You're almost through with this stuff, and then we can get on with our lives."

I nodded as we walked out the door, silently praying that he was right.

Chapter Nineteen
Genetic Testing

The following week, I went to the hospital's genetic testing department. I filled out a questionnaire and waited in the somewhat disorganized conference room for the genetic specialist. After a lengthy wait, a woman in her early fifties, with slightly graying hair, came into the room.

"Hello, Mrs. Shelton." She extended her hand to shake mine. "I'm going to walk you through the testing procedure," she said, as she examined the questionnaire.

"It looks as though you have a pretty good chance of having the BRACA gene," she pronounced, while still looking at my paperwork.

"I do?" I asked, astonished.

"Well, let me rephrase that," she backed up. "Since your sister had breast cancer at an early age, it puts you at about an eighteen percent chance of having the gene."

I glared at her. *"How is eighteen percent a pretty good chance?"* I thought.

"I know my sister had it," I acknowledged, "but her cancer was totally different than mine, and my family has never had a history of any cancer on either side. My grandparents lived into their eighties, so how can I have a pretty good chance? That doesn't make sense to me," I challenged.

The administrator sat down at the end of the conference table. "You're right. Let's just stay positive," she placated.

She told me the test would be a simple blood test and reiterated what my surgeon had already told me about it taking four or more weeks to get the results. She also went into the explanation of the insurance, telling me they would file it and hope my company would cover it.

"In case they don't, I need you to sign this form stating that you acknowledge you will be responsible for the charges." She put the form and a pen in front of me. "This test will also be beneficial to your other sister and your mother," she continued. "This way, they'll know if they should be concerned."

"Will my insurance company use this against me or them? Do they have access to my results?" I could feel the panic rising in my chest.

"They are not supposed to, but I do have to tell you that we can't guarantee it. Don't worry about it though; it's more important that you know at this point."

"Easy for you to say," I thought, picturing myself without insurance for the next fifty years.

"Okay," she said, as if finally getting down to business. "Let's talk about the results you'll be getting. If it's positive, it means that you will have an eighty percent chance of the cancer returning..."

"What if it's negative?" I interrupted.

"Then you and your sister's cancer could have environmental origins, and you are basically at no more risk than anyone else who doesn't carry the gene," she countered.

"What about my daughter? Will this mean that she doesn't carry the gene too? Her grandmother on her dad's side had breast cancer a couple of years ago." I felt myself beginning to panic again, realizing that my daughter now had breast cancer on both sides of her gene pool.

"How old was her grandmother when she got it?" the woman asked.

"Almost eighty," I replied.

"Then don't worry. A woman's risk increases with age — that's natural. But it won't predispose her." The woman was beginning to sound as if she were coming around to my side — something that I appreciated, considering I felt she had already convinced herself that I was a carrier.

I looked down at my hands and gave a sigh of relief.

"What do we do now?" I asked.

"Let's get your blood drawn and I'll send it off. We will notify you of the results." She explained that I would also get a reply from the testing company through the mail.

"It will take about three days to get it there, so give me a month and a few days; and if you haven't heard from us or the company, call me," she directed.

After my blood was drawn, I rose to my feet, said good-bye, and walked to my car. My entire future and that of my only child was now in a vial of blood on its way across the country. My legs were shaking, but I kept walking. That ferocious hum was back in my head. "*You are going to die and so is your daughter,*" it taunted. It was almost too much to bear.

Chapter Twenty
The Waiting

The next few weeks were spent going over options in my head. "It's going to be negative," I told myself and anybody that inquired about my situation. "*There's no cancer in my family tree,*" I reasoned. "*I can't possibly be a carrier.*"

I've long been a student of Dr. Wayne Dyer, Dr. Depak Chopra, and other great teachers of our time. I was watching *The Secret*, long before it ever appeared on *Oprah*. Basically, they all teach the same thing: what you think about, you manifest. I made a conscious decision that my thoughts would center on the outcome I wanted, not the one I didn't. I didn't tell myself, "*I don't have it,*" but instead, "*I am perfectly healthy; my genes are clear.*"

In the meantime, I began doing research on radiation treatments, preparing myself for the road to come. I made it a point to laugh as much as possible. My husband and I rented comedies on DVD and spent the weekends relaxing and trying to forget about the time we were really counting down second by second.

When we did discuss the cancer and my future plans of dealing with it, we tried very hard to only speak of radiation treatments. Once in a while, when I let fear get the best of me, I would broach the subject of the possibility of having to have a mastectomy. It was obvious, even though my husband didn't want it to be, that he did not want to go there with me.

"You are not going to have to have a mastectomy," he would say.

"But, Doug," I countered, "what if I do? Are you going to be able to handle it?"

Doug has a tactic he has used since I first met him. When he doesn't want to talk about something — ever — he says, "We'll talk about it later." He was doing that with me quite a bit during the course of our decision-making.

"Stacy, there's no point in going there. You are not going to have the gene, so we don't need to talk about a mastectomy."

"But what if I do?" I tried to force the issue.

"We will talk about it then," he would say, obviously relieved when I would drop it and change the subject. I know now his mind would not or could not wrap itself around the idea that I may someday be without breasts or worse, dead.

The weeks dragged on endlessly while I waited for the test results. On bad days, I would search the Internet for pictures of mastectomy patients. Although I never let Doug know I was doing that, I felt like I needed to prepare myself mentally in case the test came back positive. I had to, at least, plant the seed that I may be dealing with worse so I could hold myself together if the worst did come.

The thread to which I was clinging was already unraveling almost daily just from the pressure of waiting. After four weeks, I hadn't heard anything from the genetic testing company or the hospital. I called the woman who had walked me through the initial paperwork and got her voice mail.

"This is Stacy Shelton," I said. "I was wondering if you had my results yet? Please call me." I waited two days and heard nothing.

I called again, and this time she answered.

"I'm sorry I haven't called you back," she apologized. "I haven't gotten your results yet, but it seems as if we should have. You know, I haven't gone through today's mail yet. Do you have a second for me to check?" she asked.

"Yes, definitely," I answered, and she put me on hold.

A few moments later, I heard her almost giggle.

"We've got it!" she said as if announcing I had just won the lottery. "Hang on one more moment while I read it." I could hear her ripping open an envelope.

"You don't carry the gene," she said exhaling. "It's negative."

"I don't? Oh my God. Thank you, that's great news!" I exclaimed.

"Yes, it is," she agreed. "I'll copy these and put them in

the mail to you right now. If you have any questions when you get these, please call me. I will be glad to help you in any way. I'm very happy for you."

"Me too. Thank you for everything. I'll call if I need to," I said, hanging up the phone.

I immediately called Doug.

"It's negative," I said when he answered. "I don't carry the gene!"

"Oh, thank God." In his voice, I heard one hundred years' worth of worry, leave.

Chapter Twenty-One
Back to Square One

I met with my surgeon again to talk about the radiation treatments, and she told me she wanted me to meet with an oncologist before proceeding.

The next week, I pulled into the parking lot of a new building with big silver lettering that spelled Cancer Care. Reading it gave me a jolt.

"I cannot believe I have to be here," I thought to myself. *"Why am I here? This can't be real."* The letters stared back at me as if to say, *"It's real."*

I walked through double-glass doors and into a stark, white hall lined with dark wooden doors. Door after door held nameplates of oncologists. It was one-stop shopping for cancer.

I found the door that led to the waiting room of the oncologist I would see. I checked in, and the attendant gave me a stack of paperwork.

"Just fill these out and have a seat," she said as she handed me a pen. I sat and began answering the numerous questions about my medical history and my cancer diagnosis. When I finished, a nurse took me to an office. An attractive, middle-aged woman with untamed, curly brown hair came into the room. She smiled and introduced herself as the doctor.

"I guess we need to talk about some treatment plans," she said. She looked at my history for a few minutes, along with the paperwork from my surgeon, then she set it on her lap.

"I see that you've decided on radiation treatments. I think that's a wise choice. We have other preventatives that we can start you on too. Have you been told about tamoxifen?" Before I could answer, she continued. "It has been pretty effective, but you can only take it for seven years, and then we don't see the benefits anymore," she added.

"I've discussed it with both the surgeons I used, but I don't want to take it," I answered. I searched my brain for a way to explain my reasons, but everything sounded hokey. I thought she might think I was a holistic freak if I told her I didn't want more chemicals in my body.

"I just don't feel comfortable with the idea," I finally managed.

"Okay," she said sympathetically. "Because you caught this so early, you get to make that decision without me pushing it," she continued. "So, let's talk about the radiation treatments. Do you understand how they will work?"

"Yes, my surgeon and I discussed it."

"Then let me show you around," she said, rising and leading me out of the office and down a hall.

"This is our treatment room." She motioned me into a large white room with lots of windows. "We do chemotherapy treatments here too," she said.

We discussed a few other things, and then she took me to a desk to schedule my first session. I chose to start the following week to give myself time to get some things done at home that I had been neglecting.

Earlier in the month, I had been watching television, and I saw a commercial about a new vaccine for girls that would guard against cervical cancer or the human papillomavirus, which causes cervical cancer. I began to pray, *"Please, God, let them come up with a vaccine for breast cancer so Brea will never have to go down this path."*

I also decided to make an appointment with my OB/GYN to talk to her about Brealyn getting the vaccine. If there was something that was going to protect my daughter from any type of cancer, I wanted her to have it.

The day before the first radiation appointment, I took Brea to see the OB/GYN to discuss the vaccine.

I had been seeing this doctor for about eight years, ever since I had moved to marry Doug. Her practice was fairly new at the time, and I liked her a lot.

First, because she was a woman, and I believed that a male gynecologist had no earthly idea how to relate to a woman with PMS.

Secondly, because she was straightforward, and she took her time with her patients. It may mean extra time in the waiting room, but you knew when it was your turn, you were not going to be herded in and out like cattle.

Brea was seated on the table when the doctor walked in and sat on the tan exam stool. She rolled over to the table and looked my daughter straight in the eye. "Are you sexually active?" she asked.

Brea squirmed, then kind of choked a giggle from her throat. "No — no, I'm not," she replied looking at me like I was supposed to stop the inquisition.

"That's good," she said, "Because I want to tell you something. I'm your doctor, and I'm not going to lie to you, so you need to listen to me. Guys are going to tell you everything you want to hear. They are going to tell you they love you. They are going to tell you that you don't love them unless you prove it, and they will swear they will always love you and never leave you," she paused for a breath. "They don't mean it," she said looking her straight in the eye again. "They want one thing and one thing only — they can't help it, it's in their genes. They want sex, and they are going to do and say anything they can to get it." Brea's eyes were huge. She squirmed some more and glanced at me as if to say, "*Is this really happening?*" The doctor continued.

"If you are one of those girls who are going to believe them, you will end up a very sad and lonely young lady, because they will leave you the minute you give it to them. Do you understand what I'm saying to you?"

Brea nodded her head that she did.

"Good!" the doc responded. "I know these are different times," she continued, "but I'm really not that much older than you, and I saved myself, because there are some pretty bad diseases out there. I see them all the time in some of your classmates." Brea's eyes were starting to glaze, but the doctor wasn't through.

"You need to protect yourself, and the only way you can guarantee that you do, is to wait. Now, Mom," she said turning to me. "I'm encouraging girls to get the vaccine, and they need to do it before they become sexually active."

She went on to explain that the vaccine was given in three separate shots over several months.

"I'll get the nurse to get the shot ready," she said.

"I'm really glad they've come up with a vaccine to help prevent this cancer," I said. "I hope they will get one for breast cancer," I added.

"What is your status?" she asked, as she headed out the door.

"Well, actually, I go in for my first radiation treatment in the morning," I answered.

She swung around like a whirlwind to face me.

"Why are you messing with this?" she asked, as if stunned.

I responded, just as stunned as she was.

"What?"

She saw my surprise and walked back to her stool, sitting

down to face me.

"Stacy," she said calmly now. "You've had cancer twice in six months. Cancer comes back in two years maybe, not six months. If it came back this quickly, it's going to come back again, and if it does, it will probably be more aggressive, and you may not have the options you have now."

I stared at her blankly.

"I'm not trying to scare you," she continued. "But you need to think about it this way. Your breasts are just tissue. They are not you. Get them off. I've seen too many women — young women — die from this stuff. One of my dear friends who was barely thirty, died a month ago, and she left behind three babies. Get them off," she said again.

"Wow," I mumbled, not knowing what to say. "I appreciate you being so frank with me."

"It's your decision," she responded, "but if it were me, there would be no question. I'd cut those suckers off in a minute."

She turned back to my daughter, told her she would see her in a couple of months, and then turned to go.

"Think about it," she said, stopping to look at me again, and then she left the room.

Brea got the shot, and we made our way out of the office, my head, again, swimming. I had never considered a mastectomy if my genetic testing came back negative. The idea that it could still be a possibility had, again, just slapped me in the face. I felt as if I were back at square one.

When Brea and I finally got in the car, I turned to look at

her, fearing that she may be in the same shock as me.

"What do you think about what our doctor just said?" I asked cautiously.

"Mom, she's right." I had to stop to clear my mind. Had she really said what I thought she said? In my mind, a young teen, only three years into having breasts of her own, would be mortified at the idea. Instead, she acted as if it meant nothing.

"Think about it this way — " she continued, "what's the worst thing that could happen if you get them off? You get new, fake boobs," she answered herself. "If you don't get them off and you get cancer again, I could lose you. I'm not through with you yet. I still need you."

She had wisdom way above her years. I began to tear up at the thought that she could be left to navigate this world alone but stopped myself before she saw me.

"Okay then," I reconciled, "I've got a lot to think about, don't I?"

Chapter Twenty-Two
Reality Check

"Wait a minute," my husband panicked. "I thought you said that if you didn't carry the gene, you were going to have radiation?"

The revelation that I was seriously considering having a mastectomy was not going over as well with him as it had my daughter.

"I know that's what we decided," I told him. "But, after speaking with my OB/GYN, I think that's a mistake." I continued to tell him about the conversation we had that afternoon.

He put his head in his hands, searching for something to say.

"I just don't think it's the right decision," he finally managed. "It's too radical. It's overkill."

I could sense that he was speaking out of fear and

desperation, and the fact that he would be left looking at a boob-less freak when it was over, was not lost on me. In fact, it made me sick to my stomach, and Crazy Woman took that as the ideal time to insert herself into the conversation.

"*You're a selfish bitch*," she said to me. "*You're going to make your husband live with only half a woman for the rest of his life, just so you don't have to worry about getting cancer again. What a baby.*"

I heard each word, fearing they were true but trying to ignore her long enough to get Doug to see my perspective.

Because of my revelation after walking myself through my own death, I was determined to make my decisions based on what was best for me and not out of fear. Doug had not been through the same process, and I understood that he would need time to digest the idea.

"I won't make up my mind until I talk to the surgeon again," I said, giving him a thimble of hope.

"Good," he said. "I bet she will tell you that you don't need to go to that extreme," he assured himself.

"Look," I said, taking his hand. "I don't want this, and I want you to know this is the hardest decision I have ever made. You know that three months ago, I wouldn't even go there when it was mentioned as an option. And I'm still having a really hard time wrapping my mind around it now..."

"*Selfish bitch*," Crazy Woman interjected.

I ignored her.

"Doug," I said again, trying to get him to look at me. "I have to have you on my side if I do this. I have to know that you can handle it and that I won't make you sick every time you look at me." I began tearing up.

He stroked my hand and looked me in the eye. "I'm going to be behind whatever the surgeon tells you. Don't worry about me."

The rest of the night, my husband was quiet, and Crazy Woman took full advantage of it.

"You are going to completely ruin your marriage. I mean, get real. How many men do you know that can take being married to a woman with no breasts? You are just trying to sabotage your marriage, aren't you?"

The more I tried to reason with her, the worse she became.

"You are being ridiculous," I told her. *"Of course I don't want to sabotage my marriage. I just want to be alive to have a marriage."*

"You're an idiot," she sneered. *"Have you seen what women look like after they've had their boobs off? They are hideous, and you are seriously considering asking your good-looking, successful husband to stay with someone who's going to look like a total freak? He can have anyone — why in hell would he stay with you?"*

"Because he loves me," I reasoned.

"Well, he can love a twenty-four year old with perfect boobs a lot easier," she fired back.

"Shut up," I thought, holding my head.

"Wise up," she retorted.

Chapter Twenty-Three
Worst Fears

The following morning, I called and postponed the radiation treatments. Crazy Woman was relentless the next couple of weeks while we waited to see my surgeon. Each day, my skin would crawl a little less when I thought about having the mastectomy. Crazy Woman could sense she was losing ground, and she dug in every chance she could find.

"Have you seen how disgusting the scars look?" she would ask each time I was naked and getting into the shower. *"Look at what you've got now. Then just make great big red, festering slits across your chest, and that's what you're going to look like."*

I tried to ignore her, but it was fruitless.

"Why don't you just put your boobs in the food processor? That should make you happy," she ridiculed.

When she could tell she was making little to no headway,

she turned on the guilt.

"What kind of a woman asks her husband to voluntarily support her when she's going to mutilate herself? You are pathetic. You deserve to have him leave you. You can't possibly love him and ask him to stay with you," she reasoned. *"Just because another woman told you to get them cut off, doesn't mean you should,"* she raged. *"She's probably some sort of sadomasochist. She's completely unhappy with her own breasts, and she wants everyone else to be too. You're just too stupid to see it."*

The guilt tactic was definitely the most productive. Each time I thought of what it would do to Doug, I got nauseated. I had finally become strong enough to know that I would be able to withstand the emotional and physical trauma of a mastectomy, but I believed my husband could not. That idea gnawed at my soul twenty-four hours a day, and I came ever closer to believing Crazy Woman.

My only hope was that Doug was right, and my surgeon would indeed say it was overkill. She didn't.

"I'm considering a mastectomy," I said to her when she walked in the room. She immediately looked at Doug who sat stoic and pale-faced in his chair.

"Actually, I think that's a good decision," she said, still eyeing him.

He looked up at her as if his worst nightmare had just smacked him in the face.

"Am I wrong?" he questioned. "It just seems that it's so

radical. I mean all we've ever talked about was that if she didn't carry the gene, she would have radiation; and now all of a sudden, we've jumped to the most radical treatment?" he questioned, hoping she would agree.

The doctor sat down on her exam stool and faced him. She spoke as if she were giving him last rites.

"I know this seems excessive. But it's not. Your wife's cancer was back in six months' time. And although she doesn't carry the gene, it was more aggressive the second time around; and that means if it comes back again, it will be even more aggressive," she paused, trying to choose her next words carefully. "She is lucky that her cancer was found as early as it was. We know it hasn't spread, and that's a great place to start. If she has a mastectomy, we know there won't be any more breast cancer. We know we can save her."

He shook his head as if he understood, but I could tell that it was for show. It was going to take as long for him to wrap his mind around the idea as it had taken for me. I wanted to be completely understanding of that. It was the least I could do.

"What about getting it in my other breast?" I asked her. "What are the chances of that?"

"You are at an increased risk, just because you've already had it. The statistics say that it is probably only a twenty percent chance, and we can make sure we are diligent about your mammograms and add sonograms and MRIs to your preventive treatment plan."

I thought about the list she had just named. I was lucky

to live in a time that women had all of those diagnostic options available to them. But I didn't believe those options would make a difference in my psyche. I knew I would still spend every day of my life wondering if the cancer had come back. I paused and silently asked myself what I would do if I wasn't afraid.

"Am I going too far if I consider having both of my breasts removed?" I asked.

Again, she looked at my husband who, at this point, seemed to have checked out.

"I don't think so. I think it is very reasonable, considering your history and your age. You're only forty-one," she continued. "Your risk increases two percent a year with age. By the time you're eighty, that's an eighty percent chance you would have it again."

I sighed, realizing that the statistics had already made the decision for me, but I had to be sure.

"If this were you," I asked, "or your daughter," I added, making sure she would give the decision her full attention, "what would you do?"

She didn't hesitate. "I'd have them both removed."

"Okay," I said, nodding my head and looking at Doug. "Can I speak with my husband a moment?"

"Sure, take your time. I'll be back in a few minutes."

When she left, I turned to him. "I know this scares you. It scares me too, but I want to be around to see Brea graduate. I want to be here for her wedding. I want to see my grandchildren. I need you to be with me on this. I feel it's the right thing to do."

"Okay," he sighed, nodding. "I want you to do what you think is best for you. I'll be with you the whole way."

I got teary again, knowing how badly this was going to affect him, and wishing so desperately that it wouldn't.

When my surgeon returned, I told her our decision. She looked at my husband again. "She's making the right choice," she said. "We have great plastic surgeons that can make her look totally natural. A lot of women actually like their new breasts better than their old ones," she smiled.

"I don't want you to get big ones," he said, completely startling both the doctor and me.

"You don't want bigger ones?" I tried to make sure I had heard him correctly, because I was only a "B" cup.

"No," he said again. "Yours are the perfect size."

"Okay then," I said, chuckling. "'B' cup it is."

Chapter Twenty-Four
Square One Again

That night, I searched the Internet for pictures of mastectomy patients. I wanted to show Doug it wouldn't be as bad as he thought. As much as I wanted to prove that to him, however, I couldn't shake the idea that he would forever be cheated by being married to me.

When I was in college, I worked at a small boutique, which, along with selling clothing, also fitted mastectomy patients with prostheses. This was before the days of reconstructive surgery, and clerks had to be specially trained to do the fittings. I was not, so I never actually saw a woman who'd had the procedure. However, whenever a woman came for a fitting, the sales clerks who assisted her would take on an air of reverence. The store would go quiet, and the staff would speak in whispers as if we were in a funeral home.

When the fitting was over, the fitter would emerge with a look on her face that said she had just faced her greatest demons. I have never forgotten that, and I believed it was similar to what Doug would be experiencing.

I had already prepared myself for the worst, but he had never seen the pictures that I had already poured through weeks earlier.

The search for mastectomy pictures brought up thousands of options. I opened the first link I came to, which had before and after pictures of women that had undergone the surgery. It was true, some of those women looked better after the surgery than they had before.

Some of the pictures I found showed the procedure with no reconstruction. There was a bare, flat chest, much like a young boy's, with a three-inch, slightly red line across it. I didn't want him to see those, because I knew I would get the reconstruction.

"Scare him as little as possible," I told myself.

I moved to a page with completely reconstructed breasts and read the description under the pictures: *Fifty-one year old presented with Stage IIA breast cancer.*

This woman had saggy, baggy, frumpy and well, just plain ugly breasts. After reconstructive surgery, her breasts were nothing less than beautiful.

I was jubilant. I called Doug into our office. "Honey, you have to look at these."

I pulled his chair next to mine and patted it for him to sit down. "Look what I've found," I said excitedly.

He sat in the chair and stared at the screen. "What is this?" he asked, puzzled.

"They're before and after pictures of mastectomy patients." I kind of bounced up and down in my chair giddily.

"Really?" he asked, unbelievingly.

"Yeah. Not bad, huh?" I replied.

"Wow, these aren't bad at all," he said, raising his eyebrows. "Where were these taken? Who did them?" he asked.

"They're from all over, but we will have the chance to see pictures from whoever we decide to use," I assured him. "If they don't look as good as these, we'll find somebody else. I don't care if I have to go to L.A." I said, thinking aloud, knowing my sister lived there and we could stay with her.

I looked at Doug and saw pure relief on his face. I continued looking at pictures and realized that there were two different types of surgeries. One was a reconstruction using silicone or saline implants. The reconstructed breasts, which used this method, were very firm looking. They were perky and perfectly symmetrical. Moreover, they were very pretty, but it was obvious that they were not the real deal.

The second surgery was called a DIEP flap. The reconstructed breast was made using fat and skin from another part of the body, like the abdomen or the buttocks. That procedure made the breast look completely real, except for the scars. I decided that the DIEP flap surgery was the one

I wanted, and I made a mental note to talk to my surgeon about it at my next appointment.

"There's no one in this state that does that surgery," the surgeon told me when I explained that I wanted the DIEP flap. "The closest place you could go is probably New Orleans," she continued.

"Really?" I asked. "Why?"

"It's a very complicated surgery," she answered. "It's called a microsurgery, because when you harvest tissue and then reattach it, you have to reattach the blood supply by reconnecting the blood vessels." I felt deflated. "You also run the risk of it not working and having the tissue die. Plus, it's a very invasive procedure," she added.

She explained that it takes at least eight hours and eight to ten units of blood. She also pointed out that if it doesn't take, you run the risk of infection. "That's a whole new level of concern."

"So my only option is implants?" It seemed that every time I came up with a plan I could live with, it got knocked down.

"I'm not saying you can't have the flap. I can give you the name of the hospital in New Orleans, but the implants are much easier. It only takes a couple of hours, and we can start the reconstruction process at the same time."

"What does that mean?" I asked, not understanding.

"As soon as I get done with the mastectomy, a plastic surgeon will come in and place expanders in your chest.

When you wake up, you will already have some projection in your chest wall."

I was totally lost. In my mind, I thought I would wake up and have boobs. She was not leaving that impression.

"What do you mean 'expanders and projection'? Won't I have new breasts?" I questioned.

"No," she said, shaking her head. "There will be several surgeries before you have breasts again."

I sat dumbfounded.

"The expanders are like balloons. You have to remember, I'll be taking all your tissue and skin. There won't be room for implants. We have to make room for them by growing and stretching your skin. That's what the expanders do." She took a piece of paper out of the file she was holding.

"An expander looks like this," she said, drawing a half moon. "It sits here at the base of the breast area," she cupped her hand underneath her own breast, "and every week or two, you will have it injected with saline so it will stretch the skin. When you get it to the size you want, you'll have to wear it like that about four months before you can have the permanent implants."

"So this is going to take a few months?" I asked, beginning to realize this was not what I had bargained for.

"Actually, it takes about a year," she replied.

"A year? Why?" I was beginning to get light-headed.

"Well, when the skin is stretched, then you'll have the actual implants placed inside, and then you have to wait another four months for your nipples."

"What? My nipples? What do you mean? How do I get nipples?"

"The plastic surgeon will make them from scar tissue," she said. "Then you will have tattoos that will make it appear as if you have areolas."

This was all too much for me, and I was completely bilwildered. Why hadn't she told me all this before when we talked about a mastectomy? Why was I hearing all of this for the first time?

For the third time since my diagnosis, I felt as though I was right back at square one concerning making the right decision for myself. I was lost in a dark and scary forest with no idea how to find my way home.

Chapter Twenty-Five
Lost Again

The next few days turned into weeks while I weighed my options. I had already been through so much, and the idea of a ten-hour surgery that would mean a stay in intensive care, did not look appealing, even if it meant that the breasts would look more natural.

On the other hand, I was always one of those women who never "got it" when women wanted to have a boob job. "Your boobs are going to be perky when you're eighty," I would say. "Don't you want to look like a grandma instead of a club dancer?"

The idea of perky breasts on an elderly body repulsed me. Even more than that, I didn't want anything else artificial, especially silicone, in my body. I already had titanium hips, a reconstructed nose because of a softball injury, and colored hair. God — I would be fake from head to toe.

Several nights, I would let myself go into the gloom. Crazy Woman was doing her best to keep me there.

"Doug is going to hate fake boobs. They are going to sicken him," she would say.

I would drag him into our office and make him look at more pictures of both types of surgeries and try to make him pick for me. Then I would prod him about how the pictures made him feel.

"Are you sure you are going to be able to handle this?" I would ask. Each time, he would reassure me that all he cared about was me staying alive, and he didn't care if I had boobs at all.

Part of me wanted to forget the reconstruction all together. *"I can live without breasts,"* I told myself. But that option was always fleeting.

"He would leave you in a minute if you didn't have breasts," Crazy Woman jeered.

Then I would try to force him, all over again, to make my decision, only to have him tell me he just wanted me alive. But every time he said it, I became more convinced (with the help of Crazy Woman) that he was lying.

Some nights after going through the whole scenario, I would break down and cry. "Why won't you tell me the truth?" I begged. "There is no way you could be okay with this. I'm going to be a freak!"

"Honey," he would say, taking my hand in his, "You are not going to be a freak. I love you, not your boobs. I am not lying when I tell you that. You have to believe me."

Off I would skulk, trying to convince myself that he was telling the truth, but before the night was over, Crazy Woman had me convinced otherwise.

I have never battled with a demon so big as the decision to have the mastectomies. I know now how incredibly insane I was during that time, because I lost most of my memory about it.

I think our bodies and minds go on autopilot when they can't process something that is too horrific to accept. A friend of mine told me that her mother lost years of memory when her firstborn son died at age twenty. I told her I could absolutely relate, because there are huge periods of my own life that I just cannot place. Although I don't believe my diagnosis can even come close to the trauma of losing a child, it was hard enough that my mind couldn't keep it around.

On that note, I believe that God puts people into our lives for a reason. The year before my first diagnosis, I had become involved in a health and wellness business, which allowed me to build some amazing relationships with women I would have never met otherwise. Luckily for me, several of them were nurses. One, Pam, had been an oncology nurse. She was a great resource for what I had been going through as well as a strong shoulder upon which to lean.

Every time I had a question about my treatment or just lacked understanding of what I had been told, she was there to fill in the blanks.

Another nurse, Kim, led me to a friend of hers who had been diagnosed three times with breast cancer and had had the flap procedure. Kim gave me her friend's number, and I was able to talk to her about her journey at length. None of these ladies gave me advice on what I should do. They just gave me the facts as they knew them and let me decide. It was such a blessing.

On the other hand, when I finally made the decision to have the mastectomies, I had other friends and relatives who had no problem telling me what I should do, and it always went something like this: "You're going to do what?! Well, I would never do that!"

Those words made me seethe. Not only were they questioning the decision I had made, some of them were making me defend it.

I wanted to scream at them, *"How do you think you are in a position to tell me what you would or wouldn't do? Because I have gone over and under and around and on top of and through it for four months, and I can tell you that every time I did, I still came out on the other side not knowing what to do."*

They acted as if it were such an easy decision — as if I had given it no thought — when in fact, all I did for every second of every day was to think about it to the point that I couldn't eat or sleep.

Listening to their "opinions" made me sick. I felt the nausea rise in my stomach the same time as the anger would start to burn. Then Crazy Woman would rise up, and it was all I could do not to unleash her on them. The only way I could hold back was to remind myself that unless they had been diagnosed with breast cancer twice in six months, they were clueless. I felt so defensive that I wasn't about to tell them that I was considering having both of my breasts removed; and in order to save myself and my friendships, I began telling everyone that the topic of my mastectomy was off limits when we were together.

At times, some of them still tried to bring up the issue by asking seemingly innocent questions like "So tell me what is going on?" to which I would reply, "Oh, I'm just working and keeping busy."

Then I would see the look in their eye, which said that wasn't what they meant. They would continue later in the conversation, "So what are you planning on doing?" to which I would reply, "Well, I'm going to my company's national convention in April." Again, I would get the "look," but I didn't care. I wasn't going there with anyone again. I knew Crazy Woman was about to start telling people to take a flying leap off a high pier, and I really didn't want to lose any friends because of their ignorance.

Another problem I faced during this period — one for which Crazy Woman was all too ready to exert her wrath — was when my friends would start telling me about other people they knew with cancer. Most were their friends that I'd never heard of in all the years I'd known them, yet now here they were, and with cancer no less.

They would relate to me every horrific detail of their disease, especially the ones who weren't expected to make it or who actually hadn't. I would stare blankly at them and try to say things like, "Oh, my goodness, that is so terrible. Bless her heart." All the while Crazy Woman was trying to take over and scream, *"Why are you telling her this? Do you think she needs to be reminded that people waste away to nothing in torturous pain and then die? Newsflash: she's already been there in her head — we don't want to go there over dinner or cocktails!"*

I knew that people were at a loss for what to say, and they wanted to try to find common ground with me. They wanted me to feel they understood, even though there was no way they possibly could. I was grateful that they tried to convey that message. It just wasn't the most successful way to do it.

My nurse friends, I am sure because of their years of experience, knew they could not walk this path with me, and so they didn't try. They just let me know that they would be an ear if I needed it or a source of information if I couldn't find it elsewhere. I believe God puts people into our lives for a reason, and they were the proof of that.

I wish I could say that a luminous golden light appeared to me one peaceful afternoon to tell me what I should do, but it didn't. Hours were spent unraveling each option. Should I forgo the mastectomies all together and take my chances with the cancer returning? That option never sat on the plate for any significant length of time. I knew it would come back; I felt it in my soul, but it still had to be weighed.

Should I go through another grueling and very dangerous

surgery that would require a long hospital stay in another state and no guarantee that it would be successful? Could I leave my daughter that long? Could I afford the time it would take to recover?

Should I opt for the least invasive surgery with the least hospitalization, even though it had the most unappealing outcome?

The answer was the lesser of all the evils. I told my husband, "I'm going to have a bilateral mastectomy and get implants."

"I think you are making the right decision, sweetie," he replied, pulling me into his arms.

"Really? You do?" I sighed. I needed to hear that more than I needed anything else in the world. I had been ready to defend myself — my decision — to him and to the world like I had already had to do with others. But he didn't make me. He just hugged me, stroked my back, and told me he would be there for me. It was the greatest, most relieving moment I had since the nightmare began. That night, I slept peacefully for the first time in months.

Chapter Twenty-Six
Solving a Problem

The following week, I met with my surgeon, and she gave me the names of two plastic surgeons.

"They can better explain the reconstruction process, because they will be handling it all," she told me.

"You mean you don't do anything but the mastectomy?" I asked.

"No, the plastic surgeon will handle all of the surgeries after the mastectomies, but I will still be involved in your follow-up care."

We spoke about what I could expect in terms of future checkups. She told me they would include checking the implants every two years with an MRI. She also talked a little more about the plastic surgeons I would be seeing and assured me I would be in the most capable of hands.

The following week, my husband and I went to the first

plastic surgeon's office. We were escorted to a small viewing room and shown a video about the mastectomy process.

Finally, the surgeon came into the room. She was about my age, really cute and spunky. She looked over my file. "I don't think I can help you," she said, a puzzled look crossing her face. "I don't know why they sent you to me."

My mouth dropped, but before I could ask why, she continued. "We can't do implant reconstruction on radiation patients. Your skin won't grow back." She was shaking her head.

"Oh," I interjected, now understanding. "I didn't have the radiation. I decided that wasn't the treatment plan I wanted."

"Ohhh, okay," she said, lowering the file and extending her hand to shake mine. "Well then, that's why they sent you. No one put that in your file. It says you opted for radiation."

I immediately wondered why no one had told me that implants would no longer be an option if I had decided on radiation. Still, I was so relieved, because if I had gone through with radiation and the cancer came back, I would have no options except the DIEP flap.

The doctor was warm and straightforward. She didn't put on an air of sympathy but instead treated me as if we were solving a problem. I liked her immediately, but I vowed that I would not commit to anyone until I had seen their before and after photos. She pulled out a photo album and left us to leaf through the many pictures it contained. Although I had already seen so many on the Internet, including ones from surgeons in Los Angeles, her work took my breath away. It was much better. I looked at Doug.

"Can you believe how good these are?" I asked, wondering if he felt the same.

"They're amazing," he said, raising his eyebrows. "Wow."

"I know I have an appointment with another surgeon, but I have looked at hundreds of pictures, and she blows everyone away. I want to use her," I said in a tone that was supposed to convince him.

He didn't need convincing, however.

"I completely agree," he answered. "You could look forever and not beat her. She's the one," he said, reassuring me.

She came back into the room, and I told her we would like to schedule the surgery. She walked me through the process and showed me an expander. She began telling me about the new silicone implants and how realistic they felt, when I interrupted her.

"I don't want silicone," I said defiantly. "I want saline. They are safer."

"Not really," she countered. "Silicone is just as safe, if not safer. They've done a lot of research since they were taken off the market," she reassured.

I shook my head, "No, I don't want silicone," I said again. She could tell by the pitch in my voice that I had made up my mind. "Okay," she conceded. "We can do saline, but I'm going to try and talk you into the silicone. They are just so much better, and they really do have a better record."

"We'll save that debate for another time," I said, not wanting to take it any further.

"Okay," she said, rising. "I'm really glad to meet you. We will get with your general surgeon's office and coordinate the surgery right away."

We left and went to lunch. Our conversation centered on the procedure and the decision I had made. I carried on as if I were really present, but it was as if I were in a long tunnel, and I couldn't focus on what was happening. The words were distant and the thoughts sporadic.

I was in a fog, and I would stay there for the next year and a half.

Chapter Twenty-Seven
Saying Good-bye

The week of my surgery, Gayla, a friend in the same business as I, asked if I could help with a presentation she was hosting at her sister-in-law's home.

I met her sister-in-law, Kathryn, and learned that she was a nurse. She told me she was employed at the surgical department of the hospital where I was going to have surgery in two days. Her best friend, who was also in attendance, worked there too.

I knew this was a sign from God, or my grandmothers, or someone who was looking out for me on the other side.

I told Kathryn that I would be seeing her Thursday for my surgery. She asked what I was having done, and when I told her, she froze.

"You are here working tonight? You are so happy and bubbly?" she asked it in a question form, expecting an answer for my apparent lack of concern.

"It's good to just keep things normal," I told her. "Everything is going to be okay, and being introduced to my nurses two days before I even get to the hospital is proof of that."

She laughed. "That's right," she said, and she gave me a warm hug.

The morning of my surgery, I looked into the mirror, viewing my breasts one last time. I felt as though I should have a ceremony or something — maybe some pomp and circumstance.

The thought made me laugh to myself, but at the same time, I felt I did need to say good-bye.

I told my breasts *"thank you." "Thank you for feeding my child, thank you for giving her a soft place to lay her head. Thank you for the beauty you added to my body. Thank you for the pleasure you gave my husband."* Then I cried.

In the past, I had reminded myself that it was no big deal. It was just fatty tissue, globs of stuff that I didn't really need. However, on that day, it didn't feel like it. I realized that in three hours, I would no longer have breasts, and I would no longer be the woman I had spent forty-one years making myself. With the loss of those two pieces of flesh came the loss of much of my identity.

"What do you think they are going to do with your boobs after they cut them off?" It was Crazy Woman.

"You've got to be kidding," I thought.

"Do they put them in a jar, or do they just throw them in the trash?" she continued. *"If they end up in the landfill with the cancer still in them, can it still grow? And if it does, can it get into the water supply and give somebody else cancer?"* She knew she could still mess with me.

"You really are crazy," I said to her. *"Insane."*

The day was surreal. It was almost what I suspect it feels like for a death-row inmate to take that final walk. Fear came from the unknown, although I was able to keep it buried at the back of my brain. I had loaded up my iPod with several stand-up comedian acts, especially Ellen DeGeneres, who is my favorite. I kept her in my ear most of the morning so I could laugh.

I've heard that laughing releases endorphins that are thousands of times more powerful than the most powerful cancer drugs we have available. I decided laughing would become an everyday part of my life, even on this day.

Doug held my hand as we rode in the car to the hospital. It was still dark outside and cold, the first day of March. The darkness and temperature blanketed the landscape with a quiet gloom. It tried to inject itself into my psyche, but I refused to let it take hold.

We walked hand in hand into the surgical waiting room. We sat, and Doug rubbed my knee. I could tell he was worried. In the days before, I had updated my will. I made him make promises about taking care of my daughter and my business, and trying to keep it going for her if she wanted to pursue it someday. I know those things were running through his brain, just as they were mine.

The nurse called for me and told my husband she would return to get him after she had me prepped.

I got undressed into the sack they call a hospital gown and began listening to my iPod. Doug came into the room and stood at my bed. He bent over, kissing my forehead.

I motioned for him to sit, and he retrieved the newspaper he had brought with him. As he sat reading, I listened to Ellen and laughed. The nurse started an IV, telling me to hold still when I would giggle. Soon the nurses I had met two nights earlier came in to see me. Kathryn saw me laughing and asked what I was doing. When I told her, she, in turn, began to laugh.

"That's such a great idea," she said. The other nurse stuck her head out of the curtain and called two more nurses.

"She's listening to Ellen DeGeneres on her iPod," she said. The other two looked at each other and burst out laughing.

"Oh! We were wondering why she was in here laughing. We thought she must be crazy!"

I told them my belief about the endorphins. Kathryn became teary-eyed.

"You're amazing," she said. "I just can't believe someone who's about to go through what you are going to can sit here, laugh, and look at life the way you do."

I smiled and told her it was the only way I could cope. The nurses told me they would check on me after the surgery and said their good-byes.

Soon, the general surgeon came in along with the anesthesiologist. They asked the regular questions about eating and drinking and asked if I had any history of trouble with anesthesia. The surgeon told me I was good to go and that she would see me in the operating room. Shortly thereafter, the plastic surgeon came. She made a joke to my husband and generally put me at ease.

"When you wake up," she said, "you will have humps. They won't look completely like breasts yet, but you will be surprised at how much they will when you are wearing clothes."

That was good news to me. I hadn't really thought about how I would look during the reconstruction process. To know that most people wouldn't be able to tell was comforting.

"The more we expand them, the more normal they will become. In a few weeks, no one will ever be able to tell." She patted me on the leg and told me she would see me after the surgery.

The nurse came and began unlocking the wheels on my bed so that it could be rolled into surgery.

Doug stood up and leaned over me.

"I guess I need to give you this," I said handing him the iPod. "You should listen. She's really funny," I said, cracking a smile.

He leaned in and kissed me again.

"I love you," he whispered.

"I love you too," I said looking into his eyes.

"I'll see you soon."

I nodded my head knowing that if I said anything else I would cry.

The nurse wheeled me out of the bay and down a white hall. They placed me on the operating table, and another nurse came to my side. It was Kathryn. She leaned in and kissed my check. "It's going to be okay," she whispered. I nodded my head.

"Thank you."

That is all I remember.

Chapter Twenty-Eight
What You Don't Know

I woke up in my hospital room and saw Laura.

"Hey," she said. "How are you?"

I think I said "good," but I couldn't really tell if my mouth was working.

I drifted in and out of consciousness and awoke again to find my daughter there.

"Hey, baby," I managed.

"Ohhhh, you poor thing," she said, taking the mother role. She smoothed my hair out of my eyes and leaned over to kiss my forehead.

"How are you, sweetie?" she asked. She sounded just like my grandmother when she said that.

"I'm good. I need something to drink though."

"Okay." She put a cup under my nose with the straw to my mouth, and I sipped the water, trying to dislodge the cotton that seemed to have settled there.

Shortly thereafter, another one of my friends, Monica, arrived. I dozed in and out while she, my daughter, and Laura talked. I woke again and asked them if they had seen my chest. They said they hadn't.

I wondered aloud if we could see it.

Brea came and unhooked the snaps on the gown. We pulled down the dressings and looked.

"Hey," I slurred, "it's not that bad."

"It's really not," Laura replied.

"That's not as bad as I thought it would be," Monica agreed.

"It's not bad at all, Wuggles," Brea smiled, using her nickname for me.

I only remember bits and pieces of the next few weeks. I remember being at home and constantly having to empty the drains coming from my chest. My mother came to stay with me the first week after surgery. She would take me to the bathroom, empty the drains, and redress my wounds. I hated that part. My body felt as if I were coming off a drug addiction. I would shake like it was twenty degrees and I was naked. I couldn't stand for more than a few moments before I felt as though I would faint. Emptying the drains meant that the long tubes connected to my chest had to be pinched and then pulled, forcing the fluids down into a plastic bulb. The pulling was excruciating. I could feel them tearing away from scar tissue. If we accidentally dropped one of the bulbs, it would pull the whole tube, and I would almost wretch from the pain.

I remember sitting in our family room an hour or two a day, trying to watch television. However, because of the drugs, my mind couldn't focus; so nothing made sense.

Because my father had been addicted to pain medication, I was determined that I would not be on them one minute more than I had to. I prided myself on the fact that I was only on them five or six days after my hip replacements. I felt that it would be an easy thing to do the same after this surgery. It wasn't. I was on them for at least two weeks — maybe more — each day weaning myself down one pill at a time.

When the day came to go back to the surgeon and have the drains removed, I faced it with mixed uncertainty. I wanted those things out of me in the worst way, but I also knew what that felt like from having them during my hip surgeries. I told myself to *"grow up."* I had been through childbirth. I could do this.

When she pulled the first one out, she had me hold my breath. I yelled as it ripped through what remained of my chest cavity. The tube was long enough that it completely encased the expander. The center of my chest wall was on fire, and I thought I would pass out. When she began to remove the second one, I gritted my teeth and held my eyes shut as tightly as I could, expecting the same agony. Although it was uncomfortable, it wasn't excruciating. I silently thanked God.

The second week of my recovery, my mother-in-law came to stay. I was appreciative, but at the same time, I was uncomfortable. She was so helpful, doing the laundry, cooking our meals, taking Brealyn to school. But I couldn't shake the need I had for her to be a guest in my home and not a servant. Slowly, I loosened up, allowing her to do more and more, but I felt guilty and inadequate as a wife to her son. She treated me as if I were her own child though, and I felt immensely lucky to have all the help that we were given during that time.

I'm pretty sure that there wasn't a night that someone didn't bring us food. My girlfriends would drop in and bring lunch too. I was truly blessed.

Even when the drains were out, the incisions required two dressing changes a day. The scars were thick and red. They lay centered where my nipples used to be. There was, in fact, a half-moon type bulge in my chest. The way it stretched the skin on the top half of my chest area made it almost indistinguishable from a full circle.

After about two weeks, I had my first expansion. I sat in a chair similar to a dental chair with a small tan smock over my shoulders. The plastic surgeon came in the room and greeted me cheerily.

"How is it going?" she asked as she lifted the smock.

"Everything looks really good," she assured me. A nurse came into the room, pulling behind her an IV trolley that held a large plastic bag of saline.

"What we are going to do is to insert this needle into the ports that are in your expanders," the doctor said, as she motioned to a needle that was as large as a meat thermometer.

My eyes bugged out of
wondered how they were goi
bleeding to death. The surgeo

"Don't worry, you won't ⌐
nerve endings there." She gestureo
had on my chest.

She took a magnet and ran it ov⌐
hump. It stopped at what would be twe⌐
motioned for the nurse to hand her the n⌐
tached to a tube on the saline bag.

"I'm just going to put about 100 cc's into the
she said. "You will feel them tightening."

"Won't that be too much?" I asked, afraid of ⌐
stretching after just undergoing the surgery.

"Well, we can go less if you'd like, since it's your ⌐
time. That way, you can see how it will feel. If it gets to
uncomfortable, you can tell me and we'll stop."

She told me to take a deep breath.

"Let it go all at once when I tell you," she instructed.
"Okay, exhale," she said as she jabbed the needle into my
skin. My eyes said, "Scream!" but my brain said, "Hey, that
didn't really hurt."

The nurse took the plunger-like syringe, which was attached to the expansion apparatus, and pressed it, filling the
plastic sack. When she had reached the level agreed upon,
the doctor pulled the needle from my skin, and we proceeded
to do it again on the other side.

When I left her office, I moved slowly, trying the whole

procedure
way, it m
minutes.
By
was in
rubb
ting
e

on for size. I was afraid that if I moved the wrong ight hurt. However, it didn't — for about thirty

he time I had been driven home, my entire chest wall spasms. Every muscle was clinched tighter than a thin r band on an overstuffed newspaper.

t hurt even to breathe. I needed to lie down, but just getout of the car and to the couch was almost impossible.

I took my pain meds, and I lay in agony until they took ffect.

I stayed on the pain medication and muscle relaxers for two or three days until the muscle spasms subsided. A few days later, I began getting a burning, tingling sensation in the skin on my chest. At least I thought it was the skin. It was hard to tell if it was coming from the inside or outside, and although I couldn't really feel my fingers touch my skin, I could feel my clothes touch them. The longer the day wore on, the worse it became. Finally, I took off all my clothing from the waist up and sat with my naked chest exposed for the rest of the day. It was the only way I could get the prickly, burning feeling to stop.

Each night, I would try to go to sleep next to my husband. The movement of the blankets or his body sent arcing electricity through my skin. I couldn't sleep on my sides, because the expanders were like hard plastic bowls that wouldn't budge. They rammed into the center of my chest.

I could only sleep on my back about thirty minutes at a time, because it would begin to ache. Night after night,

I would get up and go to the couch, where I would sit with my chest exposed and watch mind-numbing television until I was so exhausted I had no choice but to sleep.

Two weeks later, I went back for my second expansion, and I told my doctor about the pain.

"That could be your nerve endings growing back, and believe it or not, that's a blessing. That doesn't happen to most people, and it could mean that you will have feeling in your breasts. Most women never feel anything again."

I was both glad and upset. I didn't think I wanted the feeling back if it meant that I had to go through the agony. I also told her about the muscle spasms. She told me to take a muscle relaxer before coming for the expansions, and we again lowered the amount of saline I was to have injected.

"The less saline we put in, the longer the expansion process will take," she warned. "Instead of a couple of months, it may take four."

Although I wanted the process over as soon as possible, I didn't want to suffer.

Before I left, I spoke with her about one final issue. I had noticed a rash on my back that appeared a couple of days after the surgery. It looked like cystic acne. I thought that maybe the camisoles I had bought to wear instead of a bra were making me too hot and that it was heat rash. When I mentioned it, she didn't seem concerned.

"Have you changed your soap or shampoo?" she queried.

"No, nothing," I answered.

"It's probably nothing. You may have a different lotion or laundry detergent or something. If you remember something that you've changed, let me know."

I let it go. Maybe it was just temporary.

Chapter Twenty-Nine
Misery

About the time I began to feel better and my chest muscles wouldn't be so sore, it would be time to have another expansion. I had not been able to drive myself to the expansions, because I still needed to take pain medication beforehand. I had to impose on my friend Kathy to take me, and it made me feel terrible. I didn't like that she had to put her own responsibilities on hold to take care of me. Finally, I couldn't take the guilt anymore, and I decided that come hell or high water, I was going to be self-sufficient.

Because I was preparing to go to my company's national convention and I needed a cocktail dress, I made plans to go to the expansion and then drop by a mall to shop.

I took over-the-counter pain medication so I could drive coherently, but I made a terrible mistake. I wanted to look as close to normal as I could in a dress, so I decided to have two hundred cc's of saline put into the expanders.

I felt the pressure more than usual when the saline was injected, but it was tolerable.

I got into my car and drove to the mall, finding three dresses to try. I was beginning to feel my muscles tighten, but I thought I could get done and get home to my muscle relaxers before it became too bad. Unfortunately, by the time I tried the last one, my muscles were in full-blown spasms. I chose the last dress and went to the cash register. I paid as quickly as I could, got to my car, and called my husband.

"I can't get home," I told him.

"Where are you?"

"At the mall, but I'm having spasms so badly I can barely breathe. Each time I take a breath, I feel like I'm being stabbed."

"I'll come get you," he said. "I've got a client here, but I'll be there as soon as I can."

I couldn't wait; I was in too much pain. "No, I'm going to come to your office, and then you'll have to drive me home. Just make sure you can leave as soon as I get there."

I had a little roadster two-seater, and it was excruciating to be sitting so low. I couldn't turn the wheel hand over hand, because each movement sent sharp stabbing pains through me. I turned the wheel, keeping my hands straight in front of me and just pushing it to the side a little at a time.

When I got to his office, I couldn't breathe at all. Tears were flowing down my face.

When Doug saw me, he went ashen.

"Oh my God, honey, what can I do?" The look of sorrow on his face made me so heartbroken for him that it caused me to cry harder and, in turn, hurt even more. He helped me into his car, all the while trying to console me.

"You can't talk to me," I sobbed.

He didn't understand why I would say that, so he tried to apologize, which made me feel even worse. I couldn't get him to realize that every time he tried to comfort me, it made my heart ache for him, and my muscles would tighten more.

"Stop, stop," I said again. "Please don't talk to me. Don't say you're sorry," I gasped. I couldn't get enough air to explain what was happening.

I sobbed the entire way home. I had never experienced that much pain in my life — not even childbirth. Every breath felt like my last. It was stabbing, cramping, vice-gripped pain that I thought would kill me.

When we got home, he helped me to the couch and got my muscle relaxers and prescription pain medication. I took them and sat as motionless as I could. Every heave of my chest felt as if I were being hit with a sledgehammer. I took the shallowest breaths I could until the medication took effect, allowing me to breathe again.

Every moment of every single day, from that point on, was spent in considerable pain.

I felt like I was going mad. There was nothing I could do to get the electricity in my chest to stop. The spasms continued, and I didn't know when they would start or how long they would last.

The muscle relaxers helped, but they left me drugged out of my head. I experimented with every way I could think of to keep from taking them. I made myself go through the agony in the day, saving them for night.

I cried, because I didn't want to keep taking the meds. I had flashbacks of my father's addiction, and I sensed I would be headed down the same path if I didn't stop. With a few exceptions, for the next six months, I could barely do anything more than stay in my house with no clothes on my chest. I was the most miserable person I had ever known.

Chapter Thirty
Alarming Boobs

Six weeks had passed, and I was determined to go to my convention in Las Vegas. I knew it was going to take some special maneuvering on my part to keep myself above water, but I needed a diversion in the worst way.

To make it easier for me to get through airport security, I carried a card that confirmed I had titanium hip replacements. It never mattered though; I was still made to go through the whole wanding and patting-down exercise. It didn't surprise me when the sensors sounded around my hips. What was surprising was when my boobs caused the loud siren-like beeping.

"Do you have metal here?" the female attendant asked, pointing to my chest.

"Um, I don't know," I answered. My mind was stumped as to what I should tell her. She continued looking at me and then turned to look at her supervisor. *"Oh God,"* I thought, *"please no strip search."* I leaned into her so she could hear me without others hearing.

"I had a bilateral mastectomy six weeks ago," I whispered. "There must be metal in my expanders."

She looked up at me to see if I was serious.

"Okay then," she said, unsure of how to handle me. "If I touch you there, will it hurt?" Again, she pointed to my chest.

"Probably not," I answered.

She used the back of her hand to pat underneath my bra area, and I saw a weird look come over her face.

"I know," I acknowledged. "They feel like Tupperware bowls."

"You're free to go," she said, looking at me as if I were pitiful.

"Well, that's a new one," I told myself. *"It's not enough that my hips go off — now I have alarming boobs."*

When I finally caught up to Angie, the friend I was traveling with, I told her about the experience. "Sorry it took me so long," I apologized. "My boobs went off."

"That's priceless!" she laughed, "Your boobs went off!"

As we were waiting to board our plane, someone grabbed me from behind. I turned, and there was an old friend whom I had dated a short time while in college. We were on the same flight. I was so happy to see him. We had seen each other a few times in the past several years, because our daughters had gone to the same private school. However, I hadn't seen him in about two years, and I knew he didn't know anything about the cancer.

Angie and I sat next to him on the plane. He plied her with stories about me, all of which I would deny. We laughed and caught up on each other's lives. The entire time, though, I was extremely self-conscious, and Crazy Woman made sure I stayed that way.

"*Keep your hands over your chest. You look like a freak!*" she said. "*If he knew the truth, he wouldn't give you the time of day. Who wants to sit with a freak?*" she chided.

Even with her insults, it was still a pleasant flight, and I was glad we had reconnected. We made plans to have lunch when we returned from our travels.

I was fortunate that several of my friends were in the same business as I, and we all had made friends with many other women across the country, including the nurses that had helped me during my decision-making process. They all looked out for me during the trip.

The night of our formal dinner, I put on the dress I had bought a few weeks earlier. It wasn't right. I couldn't fill out the top, and it bulged with empty air around the top of where my breasts should be. I had brought a little sweater that tied at the waist. I put it on over the dress, and as luck would have it, it was as if it belonged there all along.

"You look amazing," my friends told me, to which I would reply, "Not bad for two plastic bags, huh?" I would then joke that I was unhappy, because instead of losing ten pounds of boob fat, I had actually gained weight from sitting around not doing anything.

"It really pisses me off," I would tell them looking as serious as I could. They all laughed.

Each night we were there, I couldn't wait to get back to my room and take off my clothes. By five in the evening, my entire chest would be on fire again. Just the movement from walking would send jolts and sparks through me. I was able to take pain relievers only sporadically, saving them for when I couldn't take another minute, but I still had functions to attend. Somehow, I managed the trip and had a good time. It was exactly the escape from my "real" life that I needed.

On my return flight, I sat across the aisle from a woman who had been to the same convention. She was the Race Chairman of the Susan G. Komen Breast Cancer Foundation affiliate for our part of the state.

"Small world," I told her. "I was diagnosed for a second time a few months ago, and I underwent a bilateral mastectomy six weeks ago."

"Six weeks ago?" she asked, somewhat astonished. "You look great."

"I'm doing pretty well," I lied.

"You need to come do the race," she said. "You will find so much support."

I didn't know why, but it was as if she had asked me to join a satanic cult. My mind was appalled. I wasn't mad or angry — I just had the feeling that I wanted to run as fast as I could away from her. I sat for a couple of awkward moments trying to understand why I was having such a negative reaction to her words. Finally, I muttered, "I can't." I looked to the floor as I said the words. I was so ashamed.

"It's okay," she said, patting my hand. "A lot of women can't when they've just gone through this."

"Really?" I asked, raising my eyes to look at her.

"Yes, it's not uncommon at all. Just give yourself some time."

It dawned on me then that if I went to that race, I would be admitting to the world that I had cancer. Somewhere in all the preparations, decision-making, and chaos I had been going through, I had completely forgotten that the reason for it was that I had cancer.

I realized then that I had never really dealt with it; instead I had gone into survival mode. I agonized over carrying the gene, the treatment plans, having the mastectomies, my husband's feelings, my daughter's feelings — but never once had I stopped to see how I felt.

"Maybe I can do it next year," I told her.

"I hope you do," she said, and she gave me her card.

The rest of the flight was a roller-coaster in my head. "*Cancer*" echoed in my brain. It was as if I had just been diagnosed for the first time.

Chapter Thirty-One
Topless Flasher

I tried to work when I could, because I didn't want to see my business fail. The constant pain was too much some days, but I knew I had to find a way to keep going or all of my hard work would be for nothing.

A couple of weeks after the convention, one of the ladies in my business, Cristie, asked if I could assist her with a presentation. It was six hours from my home. I was not able to stay comfortable for more than a couple of hours at a time — if I lay still. At first, I told her no. But my guilt got the best of me, and Crazy Woman weighed in telling me what a baby I was; so I decided to go.

I traveled with another friend, Tammy, and we met Cristie there. The event lasted several hours, and my chest was screaming for me to take off my clothing.

Several times during the day, I would excuse myself to

go to the bathroom. Once inside the stall, I took off my shirt, and sat there for several minutes until the scorching pain subsided. Then I redressed and returned to the presentation.

When we finally got on the road, and it continued to get worse; I held the seatbelt away from my chest. Soon I was holding my clothing away from my chest. Tammy looked over at me.

"Are you okay?" she asked.

"I can't stand to have clothing touching me. It hurts."

"Then take it off," she said.

I laughed.

"Seriously," she continued. "It's dark, if we go by a trucker, cover up, but no one is going to see you," she reasoned.

"Okay," I said, because I knew I couldn't make it the additional five hours it would take us to get home. I took off the clothing and rode the rest of the way home naked from the waist up. Each time we passed a truck or car that could see into ours, I covered myself with my jacket.

A few weeks after the convention, my old college boyfriend emailed me, and we set up a lunch. He was a great guy with a terrific sense of humor, and I welcomed the chance to catch up on friends that I hadn't seen since we left school.

"You don't look any different than you did in college," he told me. "In fact, you look better." My ego was eating this up.

We talked about old friends and what we had been doing since graduation. We talked about our families and our children. I finally told him that I had been diagnosed with cancer and about what I had been going through. He was kindhearted and sympathetic.

Crazy Woman appeared to make sure I understood the ramifications of what I had just told him.

"He is thinking, 'Thank God, I did not end up with her. She has two fake hips, and now she has no boobs.' As soon as he gets in his car, he is going to speed to the nearest church, get on his knees, and say ten Hail Marys!"

"What?" I silently asked her, not understanding her tirade.

"Not because he has sinned," she continued the rant, *"but in repentance for all the bad he has ever done and the fact that God still spared him from the likes of you. He is going to rush right home, hug his beautiful wife, tell her how happy he is that he chose her, and proceed to make mad, passionate love to her while she tries to figure out what the hell is going on."*

"Thanks for that," I told her. *"My ego is now in check again."*

Telling him was a lot harder than I thought it would be. It was the first time that I had felt I would be judged. Crazy Woman brought that home even more.

I had no choice but to tell everyone who was already actively involved in my life. However, I found myself questioning whether I needed to tell others. Maybe I could just continue as if it hadn't happened. Why did they need to know? It wasn't as if they were going to continue to be in my life. I now understand it was another way I had not been willing to accept that this was real.

It was hard for me to find a way to embrace that I wasn't who I was before. I was now a person who had cancer. I was not able to sort through all of the bits and pieces that came with that. I knew I needed help.

I thought about attending a cancer support group each time I saw a flyer at a doctor's visit. However, when I seriously thought about it, I couldn't.

Part of me thought people who attended those types of help groups were weak. My rational side didn't believe that at all.

Those who can force themselves to make that long and lonely walk down a corridor to a room filled with cancer victims are very courageous people.

I think that was why I could not do it. I was a coward, and attending one of those groups would, again, have been a public acknowledgment that I had cancer.

While I had to admit it to my family and friends, I still was not ready to completely admit it to myself. Saying it had become easy, but believing it was a different thing altogether.

In fact, my friends would give me beautiful gifts with the pink ribbon logo. Kim, my friend who was a nurse, sent a gorgeous silver Brighton bracelet. I was so touched at her thoughtfulness, but I couldn't wear it. I could not announce to the world that I was a part of the pink ribbon group.

Even two years after my diagnosis, Brea came home excited one day and showed me a pink ribbon sticker she had gotten at school for her car. I asked her not to put it on.

"Why, Mom?" she asked, puzzled.

"I don't want to concentrate on the cancer. I believe in cures," I told her.

"Mom, this is about the cure," she told me. Although I knew she was right, I couldn't stomach the idea of seeing it every day.

"I just don't want to be reminded," I told her. She nodded her head as if she understood, but I think it hurt her feelings.

Chapter Thirty-Two
Trying to Be Heard

I noticed that the rash on my back was getting worse. It didn't itch, but it was unsightly. It certainly wasn't worse than the mess on my chest, but still, I didn't need one more thing making me look like a freak.

I became convinced that I was allergic to the expanders, because the rash was centered directly behind them and because it started at the same time I got them. Plus, I was allergic to artificial colors and fragrances in most beauty products. My head told me that the plastic used to make the expanders was probably full of artificial something, so I didn't think I was making too far of a leap.

The more I thought about the idea, the more concerned I became. What if the implants I was supposed to get were made of the same material as the expanders?

After a lot of research, I had decided to opt for the silicone implants. I learned, like my doctor had said, that they were in fact as safe, if not safer, than the saline. As had happened before, God sent the perfect people into my life at the perfect time. Through my business, I met a lady who was married to the man that had invented the radioactive seed procedure for prostate cancer. It just so happened that he had sold his company to the company that produced the implants. He stayed and worked for the company after selling out to them. He was with them through the implants' FDA trials, and he told me that he would tell his own wife to use the silicone over the saline.

If I were allergic to the implant coverings, would it mean that I would have to forgo the implants entirely? I made an appointment with my plastic surgeon to discuss my concerns. I told her scheduler that I needed to spend at least thirty minutes with her discussing the problem and trying to find a solution. She told me I would have to wait two weeks. I agreed.

I waited the two weeks and took Doug with me. We had to wait an hour and a half before we were able to see her.

"I am still having problems with the rash, and I'm concerned that I might be allergic to the expanders," I told her. She laughed.

"No, there's no way. I've never had anyone that was allergic to them."

Her laughter sent Crazy Woman into a tailspin.

"*How dare she laugh,*" I heard her say. "*This is serious, and how does she know? Has she seen every person on the planet?*"

"Then you need to tell me why I have this rash, why I got it immediately after getting the expanders, and why it is centered directly behind where they sit."

"Let me look at it," she said.

I raised my shirt, showing her the inflamed pustules.

"Have you changed your soap or shampoo?" she asked.

"I told you last time I hadn't changed anything," I countered.

"Well, maybe it's your laundry detergent," she replied.

I was seriously worried about the problem and I felt like she wasn't listening.

"Look," I said, leaning into her. "It is not any product that I'm using, and I don't care if you've never had a patient allergic to the implants. I'm allergic to everything," I was starting to raise my voice. "There is something wrong."

My husband grabbed my hand in a warning that I was getting too emotional.

"You sound really angry," she said to me.

"I'm not angry, I'm frustrated," I started to cry. "I've got a problem, and I don't feel like you are listening to me. You are not hearing what I'm trying to tell you."

"I just do not believe that this is an allergy to the expanders," she tried reasoning with me. "I don't see how it could be. I'm really running behind today, and I have a waiting room full of people..."

I knew that was true because of the time we had already spent waiting, but this problem was too big and it had gone on too long and I was not willing to "go gentle into that good night." I breathed a heavy sigh, trying to speak my next words calmly.

"We have been sitting in your waiting room for over an hour. I made an appointment to have thirty minutes with you that I had to wait two weeks to get — all the while, my back is getting worse. I am not through discussing with you what needs to be done." Doug grabbed my hand again.

"Look," he said, trying to diffuse the situation. "She's really having a hard time with this. She's right, something is going on that shouldn't be. We need to get to the bottom of what is happening here." I was happy that he was taking over. I knew my emotions were running too high.

"What do you want me to do?" she asked, as she sat back down.

"I'm not going to put something into my body that my body doesn't want there," I said, teary eyed. "I want you to find out what is going on. If I am allergic, I don't want to get the implants. Aren't they made of the same thing as the expanders?" She looked at me as if she couldn't be hearing me right.

"You are just going to go without implants because of a rash?" she asked, obviously disturbed.

"Are they made of the same thing?" I asked again.

"Yes, but you can't just leave your chest cavity empty."

"Why not?" I wanted her to see how serious I was. "If my body is rejecting these things, there is no way I'm going to keep them. My immune system is already shot. I'm not going to risk getting cancer or something else because my body has to spend all its time fighting silicone."

She shook her head.

"What will I look like if I just take out the expanders and not have the implants?"

"You will look concave," she was trying to get me to understand that what I was proposing wasn't a good solution. "It's not like you are going to be flat-chested. There is nothing left in there. You will be sunken in."

"I don't care," I said defiantly. But my husband did.

"What can she do to see if she's allergic?" he asked, trying to get us back on track.

"Well, I guess we can send you to an allergist that can test you, but again, I'm telling you, there is no way you are allergic."

Now I felt like we were getting somewhere.

"Then that's what I want to do."

She got up. "I'll get you the name of an allergist then. Let me know what you find out." She said as she left the room.

Doug walked me to the car, and I erupted.

"I'm so frustrated," I cried. "I don't know what is going on and I don't know if I should still have this surgery." I was sobbing now.

"Calm down, baby. I know you are frustrated, but we got what we wanted. You are going to find out if you are allergic, and then we'll go from there."

"I can't take this anymore," I crumpled into the seat. "I just can't take it." I heaved, trying to catch my breath and knowing that if I thought about the situation one more second that I was going to need a shrink. Doug started the car and began backing out of the parking lot. He stopped and turned to me, pulling my face around to meet his.

"We are going to find out what is wrong. I promise," he said, kissing my forehead.

Chapter Thirty-Three
An Answer

It took a string of phone calls to find an allergist that could help me. My implant surgery was scheduled to take place in two weeks, and I couldn't get in to see the one that the plastic surgeon recommended. I explained the problem and the time crunch, so they referred me to a teaching hospital. The hospital also couldn't help me, but the woman who answered the phone did some research to find someone who specialized in allergy testing and dermatology.

"You'll not only need to know if you're allergic," she informed me, "but what the rash is if it isn't an allergy."

Wow, I hadn't even thought of that. She called me about an hour later with the name of a physician she thought could help me. When I called to make the appointment, I told them of my time constraints, and they got me in the following day.

"The only problem is that it takes two weeks to get the results," the appointment nurse told me. "But let's get you in, and we'll cross that bridge when we get there."

The following morning, I went to the appointment. The doctor was a beautiful woman from Africa. She was tall and statuesque with a gorgeous accent.

"I understand you are having a skin problem on your back," she said as she extended her long, lean arm to shake my hand.

"I think I may be allergic to the expanders I have in my body," I told her. I related why I had come to that conclusion and how I really needed to know for sure before I had the implants put into my body.

"Let's take a look then," she said. I raised my shirt.

"Oh!" she exclaimed when she saw my back. "I don't believe this is an allergy. I think you have a staph infection."

"A what?" I could not believe it, but at the same time, it made perfect sense. It had appeared within two days of my surgery. I had to stay in the hospital for a couple of days, and I knew staph was rampant in hospital settings. A stay carried a huge risk of getting one.

"We need to biopsy it to be sure, and in the meantime, we can test you for an allergy to the casing of the expanders and the implants. We'll get both done at the same time; that way, we will know for sure," she said.

She walked me through the biopsy, which involved taking a small, but deep, portion of tissue from my back.

"I'm going to give you a local, because it is going to

hurt," she warned. She put some numbing cream on my back and then proceeded to give me small injections around the site she would cut. It did indeed hurt, but the relief I had from finally knowing what I was dealing with eased the pain tremendously.

"You will need to get a piece of the same type of implant they plan to use and bring it to me. It will only take a couple of days to know if you are allergic or not," she said. "In the meantime, I'm going to start you on antibiotics that you will have to take for at least six weeks," she said.

"Can I still have the surgery, or do I run the risk of getting a worse infection?" I was beginning to realize what having the infection could mean.

"I think you will be fine as long as you've been on them for a couple of weeks, but you need to talk to your doctor to make sure," she told me.

I left her office not sure whether to laugh or cry. I was relieved, but it was still upsetting to realize I had one more thing added to a plate already full of misery.

The Thursday before my surgery on Tuesday, I got the call that I did indeed have a staph infection. I also went ahead with the test to make sure I was not allergic to the silicone. True to my plastic surgeon's prediction, I wasn't. Again, I went into surgery with Ellen DeGeneres in my ear and laughter in my heart and a hope that this was the beginning of the end of the hellish journey I had been on for the past year and a half.

Chapter Thirty-Four
Pieces of a Puzzle

The next week was very much like the week after the mastectomies. I had drains in my chest with tubes encircling the new implants. Twice a day, I would empty the bloody fluids, trying not to pull the tubes where the skin had attached. I dreaded the idea of getting them removed and silently prayed each day that it wouldn't be as excruciating as the last time. I was determined to get off the pain medication as quickly as possible with the exception of the day the drains came out. I wanted every ounce of help I could get that day.

Having them removed took my breath away, but it was bearable. The happiness I felt from not having them connected anymore, and knowing that the final two stages of my reconstruction — the nipple surgery and the areola tattooing — were going to be much easier, almost made it all worthwhile.

There were only two other problems I was having. One was more of an aggravation than anything else. I had an itch inside my body I couldn't scratch, and I had it all the time. It was like having a feather tickle my chest wall and radiate around the lumps of silicone in my chest. I would scratch, but there was no relief. There was no way of getting to the area that itched, and it drove me crazy.

To this day, I still get those itchy moments. I want to claw my breasts off or, at the very least, stick a sharp stick into one of them and dig until I can find that one spot that screams for relief.

The other problem was that my left thigh was beginning to hurt. It was at its worst first thing in the morning. There was a raw tenderness at the same point where the surgical incision for my hip replacement had been made. It didn't really bother me much except when there was pressure on the area. It felt like a deep bruise, and I told myself that I must have lain on that side or something too long during or after surgery. I was convinced that it would go away in a few days.

During the third week of my recovery, all my caregivers had finally gone home, my husband was at work, and my daughter was at school. I had watched all the television I could stomach, and I needed to read. Reading was my best escape during those dark months.

My wonderful mother-in-law had given me a book several weeks earlier about a famous sports celebrity who had battled cancer. I wanted to be polite, but my first thought was *"Oh God, I do not want to read anything about cancer."*

I promptly put it away never really intending to read it.

In the meantime, however, Doug read it, and he reiterated that I should. I reluctantly picked it up.

Rain had gently fallen throughout the morning, and the house was quiet and cozy. I sat in my favorite chair, fuzzy blanket wrapped around me, and opened the book. Within the first four pages, I was bawling.

The author talked about how cancer changed him, and I could immediately relate.

Only those who have heard the words "You have cancer" can know exactly what that statement means. It doesn't matter if you survive the diagnosis. The fact is, you die.

The persona you always perceived as "you" is blown to smithereens, and the "old" you vanishes into the depths of nowhere. The hardest part of cancer was not dealing with the illness, the pain, the fatigue, or the surgeries. It was trying to find out who I was afterwards, and how I could make her as comfortable to me as my previous self had been. It was beyond the definition of hard — it was impossible. A year and a half after my first diagnosis, I was still not comfortable in my own skin.

I began to realize that my life had been made up of pieces that completed the puzzle I called my self. Cancer took some of my pieces and rearranged them. It took others and broke them. It reshaped those remaining, giving them no place to fit.

It was as if a tornado had ripped through my world, and nothing was recognizable anymore. I would look down the street where I had lived, but there was nothing left to tell me that it was my street.

I wasn't able to frame this new person. She wasn't me. I was taken by force into this nightmare. It wasn't my decision, but I was left with her, like it or not.

People talk about this sisterhood of breast cancer survivors. But to me it was like joining a sorority without pledging. It was as if a bunch of girls snuck into my room in the middle of the night and abducted me from a nice, sound sleep. They carried me, kicking and screaming, into their sorority house. I tried to tell them that I didn't want to be a member. "We don't care," they said. "You have been chosen."

The author also wrote about the beauty in the world that he was now able to see more clearly.

I sobbed. The metamorphosis I had undergone had also brought with it new eyes. It was like seeing the world for the first time — similar to putting on 3-D glasses at a movie and seeing things in a new dimension. Life, and the way I looked at life, had been changed forever.

I've read about people who have had near-death experiences, NDEs they're called. They say it's like waking up from a dream and realizing what you thought was reality was only a dream. That was how it was for me. The only difference was, it wasn't as freeing or reassuring as an NDE. Instead of coming back and "knowing" death is not real

— taking comfort from that and being able to live without boundaries — those of us who have been diagnosed look at events and occurrences in our lives as possibly our last. It brought a form of melancholy to day-to-day activities.

I found myself tearing up watching my daughter play the piano or seeing the stars in my backyard on a clear night. I was full of wonder for the things I had taken for granted. And, I awoke to the fact that I wouldn't always be here to witness them.

Chapter Thirty-Five
Getting Away

In the following months, I still moved slowly, letting the incisions on my chest heal. The mounds were almost funny. Each time I looked in the mirror, it was like looking at an overweight, naked Barbie Doll. There were two humps, no color, no nipples — just humps with red slits across the middle.

The scars looked eerily like the mouths of old people who had taken out their teeth, all drawn in and puckered. Upon my waking up each morning, the red slits would stare up at me. The one on my left looked like the thin slit of a semi-smiling mouth, much like that of someone's halfhearted grin. On my right was a grimace.

But, thank God, the relentless pain of muscle spasms was over. I felt like I could breathe again. It took awhile for me to accept that I wasn't going to be in pain all the time. I would wake and expect the contractions to start. I would go to bed wondering how many times during the night I would wake to them, but they didn't come. Slowly, I allowed my mind to venture to a time when all of the trauma would be behind me.

Unfortunately, October came and went, and I was still having the pain in my upper thigh. I tried to make an appointment with the orthopedic surgeon who had replaced my hips, but I couldn't get in to see him. I settled for his physician's assistant, but that appointment was still a couple of weeks away. I didn't want to wait any longer in case something was really wrong, so I called our friend Bill. He got me in the same day.

"I have this pain, and it won't go away," I told him. He asked a few questions, including if I had had any infections lately.

"I've had a staph infection for several months now that went undiagnosed," I replied.

He looked a little shaken.

"Sometimes, an infection can settle around the implants. We need to make sure you don't have one," he paused, looking at me seriously. "You don't want an infection," he added.

I didn't ask why. His look just told me it would not be a good thing. He had his assistant schedule the test immediately.

The test took several hours, and I waited nervously for the results.

His office called the next day. "It's negative," his assistant told me. I told her I would keep the appointment with my surgeon's P.A. and let them know if I needed anything else.

I went to the appointment, told the P.A. what was happening and that I had already had the scan for an infection. I was x-rayed, but he said they couldn't find anything wrong.

"Probably just a pulled muscle. It will heal on its own," he said and sent me home. I didn't like the answer he gave me, because I felt like it would have healed over the past two months, but there was nothing else to do.

When Christmas came, I was still living in a state of suspension, mostly from the reconstructive surgeries. However, I could finally see the light at the end of the tunnel.

Although I felt as if I could now make it through everything, each day would find my emotional edges still raw. Doug would say something, and I would snap at him. I think it was my way of venting all the pent-up anger and frustration I had not allowed myself to feel. He was good to let me know what I was doing and in a kind way.

"I know you are in pain and stressed," he would say, "but, I'm your friend. I'm here for you." Most of the time, that worked; but at other times, when I was so overwhelmed trying to process what I had been through, it would make me angrier, and I could feel Crazy Woman emerge. "*F you,*" she would say in my head. I would start to cry. It wasn't fair. How dare he know what I was feeling better than I did.

I had to wait four months to have the nipple reconstruction, and I scheduled it to the day. It was a day I was greatly anticipating because I was so ready to have the nightmare behind me, and because my surgeon had guaranteed me it would be "a walk in the park."

In the meantime, I started allowing myself to dip my toe in the water of normalcy again. All I wanted more than anything else was to go back to a time when I was just me and we were just we, and the most eventful thing in our day was what we were having for dinner.

I suggested to Doug that we both needed to get away. I could tell he was every bit as stressed, if not more, than I was. We scheduled a celebratory vacation to the Mexican Riviera.

"Just think," I told him. "We can celebrate that this is almost over. I will have the nipple reconstruction as soon as we get home, and we will have our lives back."

Chapter Thirty-Six
One Night in Paradise

In January, we drove three hours to catch our plane and headed for the white, sandy beaches of paradise.

We arrived before lunch and headed straight to the beach. It was overcast, windy, and a little cold, but we didn't care. We both sat under a palapa with towels wrapped around us to keep us warm.

"God, I am so glad we are here," I said, looking over at Doug.

"Me too, baby," he replied, grabbing my hand.

We sat the rest of the afternoon just watching the waves and strolling on the beach.

We learned that our vacation was going to overlap with the vacation of one of Doug's best friends from college, so we made plans to have dinner with him and his wife that night. We stayed on the beach covered in our towels until it was time to meet them.

We had a wonderful time, laughing, catching up, and cruising the shops in the little resort town. We went back to their hotel, listened to music, and had a couple of drinks before we returned to our resort. I told Doug as we got ready for bed, "This was about the most perfect day I've ever had. I can't wait until tomorrow when we get to snorkel."

About three in the morning, I awoke to a mosquito buzzing my head. The switch to turn on the lamp was on the cord, so I had to get out of bed to reach it. After I turned on the light, I sat back down on the bed. When I did, I heard a loud bang, like a gunshot.

"Oh, my God," I said to Doug, "I think my hip just dislocated."

Coming out of his sleepy haze, he bolted upright.

"No, it didn't," he said in a frantic-like prayer.

"I think it did," I said, my eyes widening. "I felt something pop in my hip, and it really hurts."

He jumped out of bed and came to my side. "See if you can stand on it," he pleaded.

I tried to pull myself off the bed, but my leg wouldn't move. It was as if it were no longer connected. He helped raise me to my feet; all the while, I would shout at each movement.

"My God, Doug — it's gone! There's nothing there for me to stand on." I winced. The pain was weird. I could tell it was there, but I had so much adrenaline flowing through my body it was muted — as if I were having an out of body experience.

Doug helped me back to the bed and sat beside me.

"This cannot be happening," we both said at the same time. I looked at him, and it was as if he had just been told his mother had died. All color was drained from his face, and his eyes were completely glazed.

"What are we going to do?" I asked him, still not believing this was happening.

"I don't know," he said. "Should we take you to the hospital?"

"In Mexico?" I gasped. "No way."

"You've got to have someone look at this. We have to have it put back in," he tried to reason with me.

"No — no way," I said. "They may do more damage than good."

We both just sat on the bed not talking and trying to process what was taking place.

I began to cry. "This can't be happening."

"It's okay, sweetie. Maybe they can just pop it back in, and we can stay here. You might be able to walk on crutches. You won't be able to do anything but lie on the beach, but that's all we were really going to do anyway."

I considered that for a moment thinking it would be great. Maybe they could just pop it back, and we could continue our vacation. The longer I sat there, however, the more painful it became. The adrenaline was wearing off, and the throbbing bolts of pain were making their presence known.

Then another thought occurred to me. There was no way I could use crutches. I was still not healed from the mastectomies. My chest muscles had been completely cut in two and sewn back together. Just the pressure of raising my arms to get a T-shirt or bra on was an agonizing ordeal. Holding myself up with wooden sticks under my arms was never going to happen.

I explained that to Doug, and we just looked at each other.

"We need to get the first flight home that we can," I finally said. He looked at the clock.

"It's three-fifteen," he said, shaking his head. "We can't do anything until morning. I've got some Tylenol. You take it, and as soon as it gets light outside, I'll find the concierge and get us a flight."

He propped me up against the headboard and covered me up. He brought the Tylenol, and I took them. Then he sat back against the headboard on his side of the bed, and we waited, neither of us talking. It was not possible that after everything we had gone through, this was the payoff.

Chapter Thirty-Seven
Crazy Woman Unleashed

At first light, Doug left to find the concierge, and I called my orthopedic surgeon's office.

"I think my hip has dislocated," I told his assistant.

"You need to go to a hospital," she replied.

"I'm in Mexico. I don't want to go to the hospital here."

"Well, if it has dislocated, you need to have it put back in as soon as possible."

"We are trying to get a flight home right now," I told her. She told me where to go to the emergency room when we arrived and told me she would let my doctor know what happened.

In the meantime, we had purchased trip insurance, because we thought Doug might have to cancel the trip to be in court. We had never done that before. I wondered if it had been an omen.

Doug came back to the room and informed me that he had visited with the insurance company representative who had told him we had to have a doctor sign an affidavit saying we had to cancel the trip because of medical reasons.

"He's on his way here now," he told me.

A knock came at the door and a Hispanic man entered.

He introduced himself as the doctor.

"You need to go to the hospital right away," he said in broken English.

"No," I said. "I need to get home to see my own doctor. I've already spoken with his office, and they are expecting me."

"I cannot release you to get on a plane without taking you to the hospital," he said. "I will be liable if anything happened to you.

I had an answer for that.

"My husband is an attorney. He will draw up papers releasing you from any liability if you just sign the medical waiver."

He agreed, and he and Doug left to have the concierge type and print the document.

We were able to fly out of Mexico at three that afternoon. As Doug pushed my wheelchair to the American Airlines check-in counter, I watched as he handed our tickets to the attendant. The man looked at them for a moment, and then a puzzled look crossed his face.

"You do realize that these tickets are for tomorrow, don't you?"

I sank.

"Look," Doug said, pointing to me in the chair and whispering so I couldn't hear. "This is an emergency."

He explained the circumstances quietly, trying to shield me from the mistake, although I heard it all.

"I've got you on the bulkhead so she will have plenty of room to keep her leg out," I heard the man say. I wanted to cry. I couldn't imagine having to spend another day in this agonizing pain.

I tried my best not to think about the trip home or how I was going to be able to sit on an airplane. I completely ignored the fact that we would still have to drive three hours after we landed to get to the hospital. I knew I had to just take it moment by moment.

We pre-boarded, and Doug held me up while I leaned on every seat down the aisle to get to ours. My chest muscles were so weak it was impossible to hold myself up, and I could feel the tension on the muscles that had been sewn back together. Tears welled in my eyes, but I was determined I was not going to cry. The flight attendants followed us asking if there was anything they could do. They helped me get into my seat, got a pillow and blanket, and tried to make me as comfortable as possible. I was silently thanking God that we had the bulkhead. There was no way I would have been able to scrunch into one of the regular narrow seat aisles.

The flight was completely full, so I knew that someone had been bumped in order to get us on. That upset me, and I said a prayer that they would understand and have something good come their way for their sacrifice.

The attendants checked on us throughout the flight. They made arrangements for a specialized wheelchair seat to get me off the plane, and a pilot escorted us through customs so we would not have to wait.

When we arrived at the airport, it was sleeting and bitterly cold. We had parked in an outlying lot and had to take a bus to get to it. Trying to get me up the bus stairs was a total fiasco. The driver had one side, and Doug was holding me up from behind. I eased myself onto the seats, keeping my leg elevated. I had to lift it with my arms to get it up, because it wouldn't do it on its own. When we got to the lot, the driver and Doug propped me into a chair in a little waiting area, and Doug went to find the car.

He was still not back after fifteen minutes, and I began to worry. The pain and the sleet were getting worse, and it was already about seven and dark. *"Please God, let us make it home,"* I prayed. Finally, when the pain was becoming unbearable from the hard, plastic chair, he arrived.

"I went to the wrong end of the lot," he apologized.

I didn't know how I was going to make the rest of the trip. I just knew I had to, and the sooner we got out of there and to the hospital, the better.

I shielded myself from each bump in the road and kept the pressure off my leg through every turn. I tried not to think about the pain of having my hip put back into the metal socket. I knew they would keep me awake for it. Each time I started to think about what was to come, I made myself stop.

I mentally could not go there. If I did, I would fall apart.

Doug kept me talking, going over cases with me, asking my opinion about juries. He did whatever he could to keep my mind off the pain. The last fifteen minutes were unbearable, and I thought I would pass out when we finally pulled into the hospital emergency room at 11:00 p.m.

"Wait here," he said as he got out of the car.

"No wait," I shouted after him. I wanted to tell him the specific instructions the surgeon's assistant had told me over the phone. It was too late though. He was gone.

Every moment became more uncomfortable, and I was searching the door for any sign that he would return.

Finally, he came rushing out and jumped into the car. "We're at the wrong place," he said.

"No, no, we're not," I countered.

"Yes, we are," he said as he started the car.

"Stop!" I screamed at him. "Just listen to me. We are not at the wrong place…"

"We are supposed to be at the North Hospital." He began driving off.

I was so angry that he was ignoring what I was trying to tell him that I hit him on his upper arm with my fist. "Stop!" I screamed. "For one damn minute, just stop and listen to what I am telling you!" I started crying.

"The doctor's assistant told me they would try and turn us away, but we are supposed to tell them that he said to come here. If you would just listen to me for one minute instead of running off when I was trying to talk to you, I could have already been in there." Now there were heaving sobs. I was so angry and in so much pain I could not control it anymore. The tirade continued.

"Get out of this car and go in there and tell them they are going to see me here, and they are going to do it now!" I screamed at him.

Now Doug was mad. "You need to calm down," he ordered.

"Then do what I told you to!" I yelled.

He reluctantly got out of the car and went back into the hospital. I sat crying hysterically.

Finally, a nurse came to the car with a wheelchair. She patted my knee, but I was having none of it.

"I was supposed to come here. My doctor told me to," I challenged her.

"We didn't know," she replied, looking at my husband as if they were both dealing with a crazy person.

She took me to a room and asked me questions about my hip prosthesis.

"I think it came out of the socket," I told them, repeating what had happened twenty hours earlier. They ordered x-rays, and a physician's assistant came to talk to us after she had read them.

"Your hip is not out of the socket," she said. She looked all of thirteen, and I decided right then she didn't know what she was talking about.

"Then what is the problem?" I asked.

"Well, nothing. Everything looks fine. It may have come

out, but it's back in now."

"There is no way," I told her. "I can't even stand on it. There's nothing there."

"That's just because your muscles have been pulled in a way they aren't used to going. You are going to be really sore for a few days, but everything will be fine."

"No," I argued with her. "There's definitely something wrong. I'm telling you it's not connected."

She shook her head as if denying what I was saying. "I'm telling you that it's just the muscles that are making you feel like that."

"Why would it come out in the first place?" I wanted her to finally see that I was right.

"You must have been extending it some way that you weren't supposed to."

The fact that she wasn't listening to me sent both me and Crazy Woman over the edge. What had just happened with my husband was about to be unleashed on the prepubescent P.A. tenfold.

"You have got to be kidding me," I snarled. "I sat down on the freaking bed. That's all I did, and you want to tell me I did something to cause this?"

"All I know is that you aren't supposed to do anything but walk when you have a hip prosthesis."

"Really? Because the surgeon — the real doctor — said that after the initial healing period, I could do whatever I wanted," I challenged. "He said I could even play softball," I glared.

"No, you are not supposed to bend over, squat, or anything like that," she retorted.

"Okay, so nothing's wrong with me," I mimicked sarcastically, "But I can't walk. How do you propose that I get around?" Crazy Woman was ready to slap her.

"Do you have a walker?" she asked.

"No," I replied in a sort of "duh" tone. "The replacement was four years ago."

"We'll get you one," the P.A. said, motioning for a nurse to do it. "Follow up with your doctor in the morning," she called over her shoulder as she left the room.

The nurse brought a walker, which I couldn't use, because the muscles in my chest were too weak. They rolled me to our car in a wheelchair and sent us on our way with prescription painkillers.

Chapter Thirty-Eight
Wake Me From This Nightmare

The next morning, I called the surgeon's office.

"He can see you in March" was the reply on the other end. I knew I could not have heard the woman correctly, because I had just explained to her that we had flown all the way from Mexico, and her office had told me I must get home and see the doctor immediately.

"March?" I questioned.

"Yes, he's booked until then."

"Did you hear what I just told you? My hip came out while we were in Mexico," I stated again.

"I understand, but he doesn't have any openings until March."

"You can't be serious," I reasoned. "There is obviously a huge problem with my leg, and you are telling me that he will not see me until March?" Crazy Woman was lurking close by. "Did you hear what I told you? My leg came out. That clearly means there is a problem, and the doctor needs to see me." I was getting louder.

"I can get you in with his P.A.," she cowered.

"His P.A? Are you kidding me? I've already seen a P.A. who thinks there is nothing wrong. I want to see the doctor. I *need* to see the doctor." My brain knew that at any moment she was finally going to grasp that it was an emergency, but she didn't.

"I'm sorry" was all she would say. I hung up the phone and looked at Doug who was sitting next to me.

"They won't see me until freaking March. Two months — that's two months from now."

Doug was shaking his head no.

"That's not right," he said, confused. "Are you sure?"

"You heard me, didn't you? I told them what was wrong. They said he didn't have an opening until then."

He looked at me as though he couldn't be hearing me right.

"Doug," I said, trying to snap him out of it. "What are we going to do? I can't stay in a wheelchair until March."

"We are going to have to get someone else I guess." He was still shaking his head back and forth, unable to compute what had just happened.

"Bill," I said.

"Bill," Doug agreed.

Bill was about to become my savior yet again.

"He says to be here at two," Bill's assistant told us.

"Thank God," I said aloud.

We went to his office, and he again had X-rays taken.

He came into the room.

"It's definitely not out of the socket," he said. "But it could be a couple of other things. You may have an infection. We will hope that you don't," he said, looking very serious, "Or it could be that the prosthesis is broken."

We both looked at him blankly.

"Bill, you had me tested for an infection in October," I reminded him.

"I know, but there's another test that's more accurate that we can have done, just in case the first one didn't catch it. It may not be that though." He continued, "I've never seen this type of prosthesis before. There's something — a notch — that I'm not sure is supposed to be there. I want my hip specialist to look at it. In the meantime, we'll get you scheduled for the nuclear scan to rule out an infection."

The words that Bill had spoken the first time I was tested echoed in my mind. "You do not want to have an infection."

"What would it mean if I have one?" I asked, knowing I didn't want to know the answer. He sighed and looked at me as if he were about to tell me my dog had died.

"We will have to take the prosthesis out. You will be in a wheelchair for at least six weeks. We have to pack the area with antibiotics and wait for them to clear everything up. Just taking the prosthesis out will be bad enough."

He explained how my own bone had grown into and around the prosthesis. "We basically will have to chip the bone away to get the prosthesis out," he said.

I sat there staring at him, going more numb with each moment.

"Let's not get ahead of ourselves though," he said, motioning for me to lie back on the table.

He manipulated my leg, lifting it and pulling it back toward my chest. I yelled, "Owww!"

A shocked look came over his face. "Did that hurt you?" he asked.

"Oh, yeah," I replied.

"There's definitely something wrong then. I have to get my hip guy in here to look at the X-rays. Hang tight for a moment," he said, leaving the room.

Doug and I looked at each other. I wanted to cry more than I ever had, but I was sick and tired of crying. I hated myself for it. I was not a wimp, but it seemed as if everything in my life was out to prove I was. I felt like life was silently taunting me.

"*Say 'uncle,'*" it would hiss, and I wanted to, but time and again, I managed to keep going. I realize now that I was in shock because, realistically, there was no way I should have been able to hold myself together the way I did.

Bill brought the hip specialist in to meet us. He pulled up the rolling stool.

"I think your prosthesis is fractured at the very least — maybe broken," he said. "But, like Bill, I've never seen this type of implant before. I want to get the manufacturer's rep in here to look at it with me. In the meantime, we are going to run a more extensive nuclear test to see if you have an infection."

He echoed Bill's sentiments about the infection.

"Let's just hope it's the prosthesis," he said.

The morning of the test I was on my way to the hospital when my cell phone rang.

"Ms. Shelton; we're sorry, but there was a scheduling conflict. We need you to come in tomorrow morning instead."

I hung up the phone, and we turned the car around to go back home. I spent another agonizing day in pain, not knowing what was going on with the hip.

The following morning, we arrived with no incidents. The technician tried to insert an IV port in my arm to take blood and later administer the radioactive serum that would light up in my leg if there were an infection present. After three sticks, he gave up and called a nurse. My veins were so covered with scar tissue from my previous surgeries they couldn't get to them. The nurse tried another six times before I made her stop. "Get the head phlebotomist in here," I said, losing my patience.

The head nurse came into the room, and the other two explained their dilemma. "Don't you worry, sweetie," she said in a thick Southern drawl. "I will get it the first try. I'm sorry," she said as she patted my hand.

She got it the first try, and I made a mental note to never let anyone try more than twice. If they couldn't get it, I was going to the head honcho.

The test took several hours, and later that afternoon, I was leaving the hospital when Bill's partner called on my cell phone.

"The rep has looked at your prosthesis. It's broken," he told me. "Are you through with your test?"

"Yes," I answered.

"Okay, I'm going to call the radiologist, just to make sure there's no infection, and I'll call you right back."

Part of me wanted to laugh and part of me wanted to cry.

I hadn't slept at all since we had been told what an infection would mean for me. I never thought I would find myself praying that my prosthesis would be broken, but that is all I had done since leaving Bill's office two days earlier.

My phone rang.

"Hello?" I asked hesitantly.

"There's no infection," I heard my new hip surgeon tell me. "We need to get you scheduled for a replacement. Do you want me to do the surgery?"

"Absolutely," I told him. There was no way I was going to use the surgeon who had abandoned me.

In the meantime, Doug wanted me to call my old surgeon's office again and make an appointment with the P.A.

"No way," I told him.

"Stacy, now that we know what is wrong, we need

information. You need to see him. Bill already said they haven't seen this kind of implant before. We need to know what we're dealing with," he reasoned.

There was nothing I wanted less, but I hoped that if I called and told them that I knew the hip was broken, surely they would let me see the doctor this time.

I spoke with the same woman who had told me before that I couldn't see him.

"My prosthesis is broken," I told her. "I need to see the doctor."

"I'm sorry but he doesn't have anything available until March. I can get you in to see the P.A. tomorrow."

I still couldn't believe what I was hearing.

"Did you hear me?" I asked, my voice getting louder. "It's broken!"

"Would you like to talk to his nurse?" she was clearly tired of apologizing.

"You better believe it," I responded.

The nurse got on the line.

"Stacy, the doctor doesn't have any openings. There's no way I can get you in before March, but you can see his P.A.," the nurse repeated when she got on the phone.

"You people are amazing." My voice was becoming more shrill. "Did she tell you that I've had two other surgeons tell me that the prosthesis is broken, and you are telling me that the doctor won't see me? This is ridiculous!"

"If there's something wrong when the P.A. sees you, the doctor will stick his head in," she countered.

My eyes bugged out of my head. I was in a total night-mare, and I had never had a real one more absurd.

"He'll stick his head in?" I asked incredulously.

"All I can do is get you in with the P.A. The doctor is completely booked," she repeated.

At that point, I wanted to kill Doug for forcing me to make the appointment. I felt so defeated.

"Fine," I huffed, so she would understand how unhappy I was. "I will see the P.A."

Later that afternoon, my new surgeon called me.

"I've met with the prosthesis rep again," he told me. "I've got some good news. This prosthesis was made to pop out like a corkscrew popping a cork. We probably won't have to chip the bone, and that will make this a lot easier," he said.

I breathed a sigh of relief.

"I can do the surgery Thursday if you're ready," he said.

That was two days away. I took a deep breath. My head was swimming. I had been so busy trying to cope with the aftermath that I hadn't had time to prepare for the surgery and my aftercare. But, I knew I couldn't wait any longer.

"Thursday's good," I told him.

I called Doug and told him to bring my will home so that I could make sure it was in order. I also had him bring my living will for the hospital.

The surgery would finally take place, fully ten days after we had come back from Mexico, and only a few days before I was supposed to have the last of my breast reconstruction surgeries.

I called my plastic surgeon and canceled that surgery.

"When do you want to reschedule?" a concerned staff member asked.

"I don't know," I answered meekly. "I don't know how long I will be incapacitated. It may be a couple of months," I said optimistically.

"You just let us know," she replied sympathetically.

Chapter Thirty-Nine
Abused

"Just stay calm," Doug told me as we waited in an exam room for the P.A.

The door opened, but it wasn't the P.A. The orthopedic surgeon held up my file, swung his hip over the exam table, and sat down.

"Well, your prosthesis is broken," he said as if he were telling me about his latest golf game.

Doug and I looked at each other, confused not only that he was there instead of the P.A. but also at his apparent nonchalant attitude.

"What you need to understand is that all hip prostheses break," he said, swinging his legs back and forth.

I sat silent and stunned, knowing better than to open my mouth and unleash Crazy Woman.

"Does it feel like you are walking on ball bearings?" he

asked me.

I shook my head yes.

"Yep, that's what it feels like when it's broken," he quipped.

I still sat there silently not knowing how to respond.

"Here, let me show you," he said, looking around for a sample prosthesis. He found it and began explaining what had happened to mine.

"We've had some trouble with this version," he continued. That triggered a thought. My right hip was replaced nineteen months after the left one.

"Is the one in my right hip the same one?" I asked, realizing that I might be facing the same nightmare all over again.

"Oh, no, no," he waved me off cavalierly. "We changed the design. See this pin?" he said, showing me a pencil-lead size piece of metal. "We replaced that with a much larger one, and we also put in a screw right here." He pointed to a hole in the top part of the device.

"I know you are using another doctor to fix this," he said accusingly, "but I want you to know I'll be happy to replace it."

Doug and I were both shocked. How did he know when he wouldn't even see me?

"We got another doctor because you wouldn't see me," I said shaking my head in disbelief.

"What do you mean I wouldn't see you?" he asked.

"I called your office from Mexico and told them what

had happened. Your assistant said she told you, but when we got back and tried to see you, we were told you weren't available until March."

"Who told you that?"

"Your nurse, your appointment secretary, and your personal assistant," I replied.

Doug looked at me, warning me to stay in control.

"We were told the only way to get an appointment was to see your P.A., and that's who we thought we were seeing today."

"That's the best way to see me," he said. "If there's something wrong, I will always see a patient."

"*Or at least poke your head in,*" Crazy Woman replied in my head.

"When could you do the surgery?" I asked, trying to be polite but never intending to use him.

"When do you want it?"

He caught me off guard. I did not want him to do my surgery, putting me into the same position of not having a doctor if I needed one.

"Let me think about it," I said. "I'll get back to you."

"Okay, then," he replied. "Just give my office a call and schedule it whenever you want it," he said, getting up to leave.

"*Big, fat chance of that,*" Crazy Woman weighed in silently.

The doctor left the room.

"How did he know we were using another doctor?" I

asked Doug.

"I'm sure the prosthesis rep told him," he answered.

When we left the office, I looked at Doug, searching his face to see if he felt as abused from the interaction as I had.

"What an arrogant bastard," Doug said.

He did.

Chapter Forty
Meeting My Match

I am a strong woman. I have always been strong. There have been things in my life that would have destroyed most people. When I was a child, I was physically, emotionally, verbally, and sexually abused. I lived in constant fear that my life could be taken at any moment.

I put myself through college, working two jobs and doing a free internship so I could make my dreams happen. I have never been a person who would even consider giving up. It was not in my DNA. Swing at me, and I was going to swing back ten times harder. I was no sissy, but I had finally met my match.

"Put me out for as long as you can," I told the surgeon. "I don't want to remember any of this. I don't want to feel any pain. Keep me sedated as long as possible. Please," I begged him.

I have never been closer to the brink of losing myself than I was the morning of this surgery. I couldn't even bring myself to listen to stand-up comedy. I had to keep telling myself that I would get through it — that it was no big deal. Deep down, however, I wasn't so sure.

After my second hip replacement, I felt myself coming unwound. I had never sat around having people take care of me. I could not stand it. I hated that I was not able to get to the bathroom by myself. I couldn't stand that I couldn't put on my own socks. I despised having to ask someone to help me do every little thing I needed to do, and by the third week of the recovery process, I was about to have a total meltdown.

I knew this surgery was going to leave me in that state for much longer than the six weeks to which I had become accustomed with the previous replacements. I also knew that because of my chest muscles, I would be truly incapacitated, probably unable to get around, even on a walker. I felt this, added to the nightmare I had already been living for almost two years, might do me in once and for all.

My wonderful new surgeon did exactly what I asked of him, and because of that, he saved my life. I have very little memory of the two months following the surgery.

I have gotten sporadic pieces from time to time of big events. I remember Bill telling me that part of my pelvis broke when they tried to get the old prosthesis out, and they had to wire it back together. I remember Brealyn telling me she wrecked her car, and my friend Karin sitting at my bedside holding my hand. I remember receiving a box of cards with words of encouragement from the women in my business — most of whom I had never even met. I remember my friends Angie and Lisa bringing my favorite cake.

I remember going to physical therapy and trying to get through the waiting room on my walker. I took a step and felt a muscle under my right arm snap. I yelled in pain. It had ripped and pulled away from my chest wall. I couldn't walk any further using the walker and had to be taken to the physical therapy room by wheelchair.

I remember trying to pull my leg two inches off the platform where I lay. I couldn't do it. I remember asking myself if I would ever be able to walk again and suspecting I wouldn't.

I remember realizing that the business I had given my heart and soul to for the past two and a half years was not going to survive, because I could not work it.

And, I remember asking God if I was a bad person and if that was why I was being punished so severely.

Chapter Forty-One
A Picture's Worth

Time seemed to stand still for me in the following months. Each day was a battle just to survive. It reminded me of the movie *Groundhog Day*. I would wake knowing that nothing was going to change this day. I would still not be able to get around by myself. I would still be stuck at home. If I managed to walk at all, it was going to hurt my chest.

I couldn't stand being so pathetic, and I sent everyone who was helping me home. I convinced myself I could get back and forth to physical therapy by myself. I tried it for two days. I was so exhausted I couldn't even get myself to my car without stopping in the waiting room and resting for several minutes. Then I would have to sit in my car in the parking lot until I could get my throbbing chest muscles to settle down enough to be able to operate the steering wheel. Plus I couldn't do the therapy without taking pain medication that left my head foggy. I finally asked my doctor to release me and just let me do the exercises from home.

"I've been through the hip replacement drill twice already," I told him. "I know what I'm doing. Please just let me stay home." He reluctantly agreed.

My calendar was full of doctor appointments. If I wasn't seeing the general surgeon, I was seeing the plastic surgeon. If I wasn't seeing the orthopedic surgeon, I was seeing my gynecologist.

Since a few months after the mastectomies, my periods had gone crazy. I was used to having a five-day, normal-to-light flow my entire life. Now they were raging, gushing floods that only lasted two to three days.

"Your hormones are very different now," the OB/GYN told me. "We store estrogen in our fatty tissue, especially our abdomen and breasts. You don't have breasts now, so your estrogen is different."

We talked about procedures I could have to stop the bleeding, but there was no way I was going to undergo any more surgeries. I still had my nipple reconstruction looming on the horizon, and I wanted that to be the last surgery I would ever have.

In the meantime, I was doing everything I could to keep from becoming depressed. It had only taken me six weeks after my previous hip surgeries to get off the walker and move to a cane. It had been two months, and I was nowhere close to leaving the walker behind. Again, God sent the right people into my life at the right time.

A year or so earlier, I had regained contact with Ray, a retired architect I had known before I moved and married Doug. He was a casual acquaintance and a very nice man.

When Brealyn was very young and suffering from bouts of pneumonia and asthma, he brought an air purifier to our home. That act of kindness touched me so much — that someone that I really didn't know well went out of his way for my child.

When a mutual friend of ours sent me an email one day, I saw his name on the list of recipients and got in touch with him. He had taken up photography as a hobby. He put me on his email list and began sending me wonderful pictures of birds, flowers, and wildlife that he shot around the lake near his home.

We shared a love of bird-watching, and he sent some of the most amazing and often funny pictures of the little feathered creatures. I began to look forward to the pictures every day. I would look at them right before going to bed so that I could go to sleep smiling. Each day, I awoke anticipating another beautiful moment captured by his lens.

I wrote him a letter telling him how grateful I was for the pictures and trying to explain what they had done for me. I don't think, however, that he will ever really know how powerful they were.

They were a momentary escape from the horrific life I was leading and one of the very few things that could make me smile during that long and dark time.

"Reflections," one of the many photos shared
with the author by photographer, Ray James

Chapter Forty-Two
One Prayer Answered

In March, we had another setback, in a long line of setbacks. Brealyn had been having stomach problems since she was very small. I had taken her to several specialists who ran tests, only to come up empty-handed.

She would go through bouts where she couldn't eat anything except saltine crackers. She was constantly nauseated and vomited on a daily basis. Then, after a few months, it would subside and she would return to normal.

Because ulcers ran in our family, the doctors and I thought that was the problem. They treated her with ulcer medication, but to no avail. Because she constantly was fighting whatever this problem was, her immune system was stretched, and she stayed ill. If a cold or stomach virus was going around, she would get it. She missed weeks of school because of illness.

To make matters worse, she was unable to take antibiotics. They made her doubly ill and left her vomiting even months after she discontinued using them.

One weekend, she began complaining that her stomach was hurting her again. I gave her ulcer medication, but an hour later, she was worse.

"Mom, I really think I need to go the hospital," she said.

That scared me, because even though she would complain of the nausea on a daily basis, she never said she wanted to go to the hospital. I took the conservative route, however, and took her to an urgent care clinic.

They gave her a gastrointestinal cocktail, saying that if it was an ulcer, the pain would subside in a matter of moments. However, the longer we waited for it to work, the worse her pain became.

"You need to take her to the emergency room," the clinic physician told me.

I was still on the walker, and it was everything I could do just to get myself into the clinic without ripping the chest muscles again. I was in complete turmoil as to how I was going to get her around. I told myself that it didn't matter — I was going to do whatever I had to.

When we arrived, she was checked in and taken down a long hall. "Just go find out what's wrong with her," I told the nurse as she turned around multiple times to wait on me to catch up with them. "I'll be there as soon as I can."

I was about to cry. I knew she wanted me to be with

her, because she was scared. I could see it in her eyes. I was scared too, but I couldn't go any faster. My legs and chest were completely fatigued.

Finally, I made it to her room while the nurse was drawing her blood. The doctor arrived and ordered chest x-rays to check for a blood clot in her lungs and an ultrasound to check her gallbladder. Again, we had to make our way down another long hall to an X-ray room. I sent Brea and the nurse ahead, knowing I couldn't keep up with them. By the time we went back to her room, I thought I wouldn't be able to make it another step. It took me twenty-minutes of shuffling before I got there.

As before, the medical staff could not diagnose what was wrong with her, and after a few hours, she was sent home with pain medication. They told us to follow up with her regular doctor on Monday.

I had just recently found a new doctor for both of us, because I needed a general practitioner, and Brea had outgrown her pediatrician. Brea wanted a female doctor because she was modest. I wanted one because of all my breast issues. This doctor was a young mother, vibrant and extremely caring. And best of all, she listened — really listened. She was a perfect fit for us both and we loved her.

"I guarantee it's her gallbladder," she said less than one minute after I told her Brealyn's symptoms.

"They did an ultrasound that said her gallbladder was fine," I questioned.

"Ultrasounds aren't really that great. There is a scan that

is much more accurate," she said confidently.

Brea had the scan, and sure enough, her gallbladder was only functioning at eighteen percent. I was floored. This child had spent almost ten years with the problem, and the finest specialists in our state had never even looked at her gallbladder. As a mother, I was crushed, and I was angry. I was angry that I had failed her, and I was crushed that she had needlessly lived in pain for most of her life.

"*I should have demanded that they find out what was wrong with her*," I told myself. "*Instead, I just let them send her home time and time again.*"

I had gotten numb to her complaints. I had let her live all those years, like I was having to live now. I have never felt more like a failure in my life than I did then.

When Brea's gallbladder was out, I had a completely different child on my hands. She had color in her face where there used to be paleness. She had a sparkle in her formerly dull and listless eyes. And best of all, she could eat and not throw up. She was happy, spunky, and beautiful — all the things that I had forgotten she could be.

"I just can't believe you diagnosed her within five minutes," I said to her doctor at her next visit. I told her of my guilt and that I felt I had failed as a mother.

"No, you can't think that way. It's rare that a child of her age has this problem. It's usually only in Native American girls that we see the problem this young."

A light bulb went off in my head. Brea was part Native

American. It was an extremely small part, but it still could have been the reason. I did feel better though knowing that there was a reason she hadn't been diagnosed before. I will always owe her doctor the greatest debt of gratitude for finally putting an end to my daughter's pain.

Chapter Forty-Three
A Night to Remember

Spring was coming, and I was anxious to leave the walker behind. The surgeon told me I could do it when I felt strong enough; and at six weeks, I tried. But there was no strength in my leg at all. It felt as if I were walking on a sponge. Each step left me lunging to grab hold of something steady, and I would re-rip the muscles in my chest. I was so frustrated day after day when I was still seeing no progress.

I wanted to coach softball again. I had to lie out the summer before because of the mastectomies. It was the first time in ten years that I hadn't coached. I missed it and the girls badly. I was determined that even if it meant I was in a wheelchair, I would be on the field that year. I knew having a purpose was the only thing that would stop me from plummeting into the blackness trying to claim my soul. It was going to be the buoy that kept me afloat.

When the season started, I was still on the walker, but I was happy. Most of the girls I had been coaching in the past wanted to play again. We started practices, with me sitting on a stool on the sidelines. After practice, they would gather the gear and throw it in my car. Then they would help me get to it.

Four months after the surgery, we started our season. During the day, I was still using the walker, but I was determined to coach the games with nothing more than a cane. On game days, I would practice walking with the cane in my house. I learned that if I leaned heavily on the cane and shuffled my feet instead of lifting them that I could get around. I knew I wouldn't be able to do it all the time, but the idea of showing up at the ball field on a walker was too humiliating. It was bad enough just to show up on a cane.

When I finally got to use the cane full-time, it caused an additional problem. I gripped it so tightly that the muscles in my right hand and arm would spasm and cramp most of the night. When I awoke in the morning, my fingers were locked into a fist. I would have to pry them open and massage them before they could move on their own. The muscle that had torn in my chest was also suffering. It felt as if it were hanging loose from my side. When I lifted my arm, it was as if I had something inside me, dangling. I started wearing a tight sports bra to hold it in place.

Coaching softball was the best prescription pain medication I had. It brought me back into reality. It gave me something else to think about besides my own pathetic existence.

It was a marvel watching these girls, who were now young women, come into their own. We took second in the league, and we would have taken first, but because of rained-out games, we had to play our tournament in three days. On the final day, we played three games back to back with only ten-minute breaks. The last game was for the championship, and my pitcher had already pitched fourteen straight innings. We were short players, so each girl played all fourteen innings. Then we had to play another seven with no dinner break. We were on the field over five hours that night.

It was a heart-breaking game. We let the opposing team run away with the first inning before taking back control over the following six. The problem was that my girls were exhausted and injured and they couldn't get their offense back together. Although we lost, they never gave up.

Hailey, my pitcher, was still striking girls out in the twentieth inning. Nikki, my catcher, had spent hours squatting behind the plate, but was still managing to make plays. Becca, my left fielder, had taken off all the skin on her sliding thigh, but she continued to slide. Hannah, the shortstop, was catching drives hurtling toward her shins and tagging the runner out. The rest of the infield, Brea, Anna and Mollie, were causing their opponents to drop like flies. Brea, at first base, had five outs and Anna, at second, had four. The outfielders, Pam, Taylor, Becca and Tristan were catching fly balls that should have been home runs. Watching them, I realized that the culmination of all the years we had spent together on the field, had made every player on the team a superstar. It was a thing of beauty.

We topped off the evening having breakfast at an all-night diner. It was one of the greatest nights of my life.

Then it was over.

The author's softball team, "The Mob"
Front row, l-r: Brealyn, Hannah,
Hailey, Kira, Anna, Nikki and Pam
Back row, the author, Mollie, Taylor,
Katie, Becca and Tristan

Chapter Forty-Four
Exciting Nipples

Almost six months had passed, and I could tell that I was finally getting to a point where I could reschedule my reconstructive surgery. My leg was healing enough that I didn't have to be on a cane all the time. I had even been able to make short trips to the grocery store without it, especially if I could use a cart to hold my weight.

The idea of having the final surgery gave me newfound hope. I scheduled it, giving myself a few more weeks so that I could build enough strength to get rid of the cane for good.

The night before my surgery, I downloaded more stand-up comedy to my iPod. I found great comfort in knowing I could laugh before I was about to be cut open. It made me forget about my fears, and I could tell it eased Doug's tension too. He would sit next to my bed reading the paper and look over the top at me when he heard my giggles. He would smile too.

As we readied ourselves for bed that night and lay in the stillness, he caressed my hair.

"Are you excited about getting your nipples?" he asked.

I stalled, trying to get my brain around what he had just asked, then I laughed. It sounded so absurd.

"Oh — nipples; I'm getting nipples — that's right. Am I excited? Hmmm. Excited. Hmmm," I said, wrestling with the thought that nipples should make me excited.

"Are nipples something to get excited about?" I asked, wondering aloud.

"I don't know," Doug answered. "I just thought you might be excited." He thought the question was for him when, in fact, I was asking myself.

"Well, I haven't really thought about it," I said, propping myself up on a pillow. I pondered some more.

"Yeah," I finally answered. "I think I am excited about it. It means I'm one step closer to losing the Barbie boobs," I paused. "Yes, I am definitely excited about getting nipples. Nipples are good," I declared.

He smiled, amused at the process through which I had gone.

"I'm glad for you." He kissed my nose sweetly. But then Crazy Woman butted in.

"He's not glad for you — he's glad for him. He's sick and tired of being with a woman with Barbie humps and no nipples. He thinks you are a freak — and you are a freak,

you know. You walk around looking like you have real boobs, but God forbid you ever flash anyone. They would run away screaming. You could be in the freakin' circus, for God's sake."

"*Ugh,*" I rolled my eyes, wishing I could slap the evil little witch that lived inside my head. "*I'm not listening,*" my head voice replied. "*Not listening, not listening, not list...*"

"*Too late — I know you heard me.*"

I ignored the last statement, kissed Doug goodnight, and rolled over on my side watching the candle I had lit dance to its shades of orange and blue.

"*Nipples are good,*" I thought and then drifted to sleep.

My plastic surgeon was true to her word. The nipple reconstruction was a walk in the park compared to the previous surgeries.

Before the surgery, she placed EKG stickers on my chest. They had the little metal snaps like those found on blue jeans. As crazy as it sounds, the stickers looked like an areola and the snaps like a nipple.

"How about there?" she asked Doug and me after she placed the first ones.

"I think that's too high," I said, looking in the mirror.

"No," Doug interjected. "That looks right."

"No, it's too high," I disagreed.

The surgeon interrupted. "Let's just move them a little then," she said, removing the first two stickers and replacing them with two more.

"More to the right," I told her, after she placed one on my right breast.

We went back and forth a couple of more times before I thought they were just right.

"You are not going to believe how much of a difference the nipples will make," she said to Doug. Then she turned to me. "This is the part when they really look like breasts."

I went home the same day with bandages covering my chest. I changed the dressing on them twice a day, putting a thick white layer of Silvadene cream over the wads of flesh and covered that with a clear plastic shield that looked like a shortened baby bottle nipple. I had to wear them for several weeks until all the stitches had dissolved.

On the day I finally got rid of the bandages, I showered and dried off in front of my bathroom mirror. Staring back at me were the two protruding mounds of flesh. I had nipples. The surgeon was right. I couldn't believe the difference these two small globs made. I saw what looked like real breasts for the first time in over a year.

When I was released from the bandages and nipple shield, I was given a large foam donut, which wrapped around the nipple to protect it. I wore that another six weeks.

As the weeks passed and they healed, my breasts became more a part of me. I wasn't shocked every time I saw my naked chest. The only thing missing was the color around them. I didn't want to wait the three months it would take to get my tattoos. I wanted to know right then if all I had been through was going to be worth the sacrifices I had made.

I decided to make an areola myself. I took a lip pencil and drew a circle around the makeshift nipple. Then I filled it in. I gasped when I looked into the mirror. A smile gleamed across my face. These pouches of silicone, stretched skin, and twisted scar tissue looked better than my real breasts had. I cried.

I called Doug and Brea into the bathroom to look too. They both laughed.

"They're too pink!" Brea squealed.

"I don't care," I said. "They are beautiful!"

Chapter Forty-Five
Losing What I Finally Found

My father died a month after my nipple reconstruction surgery. He was just weeks shy of seventy-three. He was the epitome of a grumpy old man.

In the previous two years, he had to undergo dialysis because a blockage in the artery to his kidneys caused them to fail. Three times a week, he spent four hours hooked to a machine that filtered his blood. It seemed that at least once a week, or at the very least once a month, some kind of havoc was wreaked because of those treatments.

For a while, I drove him to his treatments. We often spoke of the fact that no one understood how incredibly depressing and mentally and emotionally debilitating it was to be in constant pain. I, for the first time in my life, finally understood why he had always been so angry. Looking back at all he had endured during his lifetime, I could now see why he had turned to alcohol and narcotics.

When he was eighteen, he was told he wouldn't live past thirty because he had to have three-fourths of his stomach removed for a bleeding ulcer. He lived with permanent paralysis because of a broken neck in his early forties. It ruined a brilliant career and sent him into early retirement, leaving him with chronic back and neck pain for the rest of his days. He also had multiple seizures and subsequent back surgeries because of the injury.

Finally, he lost his kidneys, and as a side effect, battled congestive heart failure and pneumonia relentlessly. After going through the twenty-nine months I had just endured, it was now easy for me to understand him.

As a child, seeing what the drugs had done to him, I had made a conscious decision to try to never take pain medication unless I had no choice. I never drank more than a glass of wine once or twice a month.

However, I learned very quickly during my expansion process and the prosthesis failure, that given the right circumstances, I could have succumbed to anything that would help me numb the discomfort. Every day, I was just hanging by a thread.

The last conversation I had with him was just hours before he died. Again, he was angry. He was complaining about my mother — whom he had divorced some twenty years earlier — getting into his household affairs. But, instead of begrudging him those feelings, I learned to see them for what they were — a release of all the hurt, all the frustration, and all the anger at what he had to endure. And I was aware for the first time that he was scared.

It made me love him all the more, because for the past two years, I had been right there with him. He was the only person I knew who could really, truly relate to what I had been through. It was also during that time that I learned to admire him, because he lived some fifty years with his suffering, and I didn't think I could take it one more day.

My heart broke into little pieces at his funeral. The years of living in fear of him had melted into puddles of sympathy and compassion. When my dad died, he took one more piece of me with him.

The author's father, Billy L. DePrater

***

Our family had never been close. I had severed ties with my oldest sister shortly after I got cancer. She was an extremely negative person. I tolerated her as long as I could, but I came to the realization that I no longer wanted that kind of person in my life. I believed life was too short to be around people who make you miserable, and I wasn't doing anybody, especially myself, any favors by keeping the relationship alive.

My dad had been the only real glue that kept me with a connection to most of my family. My siblings and my mother still had a relationship with him, several of them being caregivers. But with his absence, the one commonality we had was gone.

Although my mother was still living, I hadn't really looked at her as my mother in decades. That role had been played by my grandmothers.

My dad and I often talked about the relationship I had with my mother. I never understood it, because since Brealyn had come into my life, my own daughter was the thing that mattered to me the most.

My birth had the opposite effect on my mom. She and my father lived in New Jersey at the time. When I was six months old, she sent me to live with her mother in Oklahoma. When I was grown, I asked her why. She said she didn't like me when I was a baby because I was too demanding.

I was the forth of five children, and she became pregnant again with my brother shortly after my birth. I know she was overwhelmed, but the pain of hearing the words she "didn't like me" still resonates with me today.

My parents retrieved me when they moved back home, but it was my grandmothers who remained my caregivers most of the time.

Even after we were grown and gone, my mother would often tell me, "If I had it to do over again, I wouldn't have had you kids." Similar to hearing that I was unwanted as a baby, those words would make me die inside. I walked away feeling as if my existence was a huge mistake.

In fact, at times, I felt as though I deserved the cancer — as if I had asked for it in some way by being such a disappointment to her.

My dad, although he had been abusive to us when we were young, made amends. When he became sober eighteen years before he died, he came to me one night at my home. We sat across from each other at my dining room table, and he said, "I know I've been a bad father, and I know my drinking caused you a lot of pain and harm, and I want you to know I am sorry for all of it. If I could take it back, I would." In that one tiny instant, every hurt, every pain, every disappointment melted, and I loved my dad.

My mother never did that. In fact, when I told her how she had made me feel — how long I had to go to counseling just to process her words — her reply to me was, "You just need to get over it."

Cancer opened my eyes to all the toxins in my life. My mother was one of them, and with my father's death, I chose to walk away from her too.

Chapter Forty-Six
Furry Solace

The weeks after Dad's death turned hellish for me. I was teetering on the edge of a deep depression — becoming a person I never wanted to be. I found myself in crying jags five or six times a day. I was devastated that I had finally gotten to break down the wall that had kept me separated from my dad, and now he was gone. I was no longer able to hold back any of the sorrow my soul had been wrapped in for the previous two and a half years. Any reminder of him or the cancer sent me into a black hole.

One rainy afternoon, needing an escape, I walked into a video store to rent comedies. As I waited in line to pay, I saw a candy display of pink M&Ms. The proceeds were going to the Susan G. Komen Foundation. There in line I began to tear up. "*Stop,*" I told myself. "*Why are you getting emotional about pink M&Ms?*" I scolded. I paid for the rentals, got in my car, and began to cry. It had just become apparent to me I would never escape the constant reminder of this stupid disease until, like my father, I was returned to the earth.

I cried because of that realization and because of the understanding that the grumpy old man I called "Dad" had to face his mortality every day of his life, and that was no way to live.

Before my father passed, I made plans to adopt a dog that belonged to a friend of ours. I had never considered myself a dog person, but Doug had wanted one for some time. I fought him as long as I could, but on his birthday the previous year, I gave in and let him get one from a local "no kill" shelter. His name was Teddy, and he was a great dog, but he was clearly Doug's.

I first saw Maxwell earlier in the summer. He was a fifty-pound tub of gray fuzz. He looked like a miniature sheep dog, and he was the cutest thing I had ever seen. I jokingly told his owners I wanted him.

To my surprise, a few weeks later, they offered to let me adopt him. Max had been staying outdoors, but he was allergic to grass. In fact, his hind end was hairless because of the allergies. They didn't want an indoor dog but felt it was unfair to keep him outside. I was more than happy to take in the boarder.

The day we buried my father, Brea and I went to get him. My heart was weary and tired that evening, but the moment I saw him, it skipped a beat.

Max cried when we took him, a long and sorrowful howl. It broke my already broken heart. But I assured him he would grow to love us and that I would rescue him from his life outdoors; in reality, he rescued me.

From the beginning, he followed me everywhere I went, staying at my feet, and by the second day, I was head over heals in love with him.

He was amazingly loving and compassionate. Each day that I found myself mourning my father, he would place his paw on me, offering me the comfort I couldn't find elsewhere. His presence was nothing short of magical.

In the past, I had heard of people who had panic attacks, and I would just shake my head, thinking how crazy that was. But when I had to leave my house, I became agitated — being outside those walls brought on an overwhelming sadness. I was uncomfortable in my own skin, not knowing how to help myself or how to regain even the tiniest part of who I was. All I could think about was getting back home.

As soon as I did, Max would be at the door waiting. Brea told me the moment I left, he would lie against the door listening for my return. She said the look on his face was one of pure, heartwrenching sadness.

When I had to leave Max, I also felt the heartwrenching sadness, but it was mine. There was something about him that was healing. Just seeing his crazy, Albert Einstein-like eyebrows cracked me up. He was the only thing that eased my suffering, and I finally understood the reason for the attacks. When I was away from him, my pain returned.

It was as if Max had been shielding every raw nerve in my body. When I wasn't with him, the shield was removed, and I could feel it all again. Absence from him was absence of joy.

Max's first owner, Becky, had died of cancer. His second "mom," Becky's cousin, Lynette, told me that Max stayed by Becky's side for three days without leaving to eat, drink, or go to the bathroom. The moment Becky passed, Max left.

When I looked into his eyes, I could see that he had lived through as much pain and loss as I had. That, coupled with the fact that he had a problem with his left leg, leaving us both limping around the house together, confirmed that we were kindred spirits.

Sometimes life's bandages come in the most surprising packages.

Maxwell "Buppy" Shelton

Chapter Forty-Seven
Great Mistakes

By September, the trauma of our lives had finally caught up to Brealyn. She was sullen, impatient, unhappy, and rebellious. Because of the hip injury, I had been physically absent from her life for several months. Because of the cancer, I had been mentally absent for two years. Every moment of every day before the illness had been about her.

Also, when she turned sixteen and got her license, our separation was exacerbated because she no longer needed me to chauffer her. The moments we had spent together in the car were times that we connected. She would lose herself, forgetting it wasn't cool to talk to a mom. The walls came down, and she would spill all the details of her life. They were precious moments — the only ones we had, it seemed, to stay connected. When she was handed her driver's license, I was handed my walking papers.

For her, I think my dad's death was the straw that broke the camel's back. She had suffered through the loss of her uncle and grandmother, my cancer and my hip failure, all without much fallout.

I told her that she needed to acknowledge her feelings regarding what she had been through, but she always said she was fine. It became clear that she never really dealt with it, and like most emotional baggage, it was going to find a way to be recognized. She could no longer contain it, and all hell broke loose.

After my second diagnosis, Brea began dating a boy two years her senior. I wasn't happy about it, but I trusted that she would tire of him quickly. I was also in no place physically or emotionally to fight her.

She didn't tire of him, however. She fell head over heels in love with him, and he became more of an influence in her life than her father and I.

Shortly after my dad's death, her boyfriend began making some bad decisions, and we saw they were starting to rub off on her.

I made two horrible mistakes where she was concerned. First, I took the coward's way out. When she wanted to do something that I didn't think she should, I let her anyway, because it was easier not to have the stress of an argument.

Secondly, instead of incorporating the lesson I had learned, I regressed and began making decisions out of fear. I became convinced that if I didn't allow her to spend as much time with him as she wanted, she would end up sneaking off and marrying him.

Those two mistakes almost led to her demise. The more time she spent with him, the more sullen and resistant to our rules she became. His bad decisions were starting to look good to her, and things that she would have never tolerated in a relationship were now becoming acceptable to her.

He had dropped out of school, and she began telling me she was sick of school and wanted to quit. She was a straight-A student, and her father, Brian, and I were not about to let that happen.

"You need to examine why all of a sudden you think these things that you have always said you would not put up with from a boy, you are now defending," Brian, said to her.

"You just don't like him," she retorted.

"You used to say you would never date someone who smoked," he tried reasoning with her, "but now you say it's okay. You are losing your true identity Brealyn," he countered.

She was having none of it. For every concern, she had a defiant answer.

"I want to be on my own!" she yelled. "I can take care of myself. Why won't you let me?"

"Because you are seventeen," I tried reasoning with her.

"I can finish school online and work full-time. I can support myself."

"It's not going to happen, Brea. You might as well stop asking," I told her.

The moment she came home from school, she would start in about how she was sick of living with us and wanted to be on her own.

I didn't know what to do. The stress of it all was becoming so overwhelming I felt I was only moments away from a psych ward.

"Brea, you have to stop this. I can't take anymore," I pleaded with her. "How much do you think one person can go through? I just lost my dad. Please stop. Be patient, you will be out of school soon. Bide your time," I begged. My words continued to fall upon deaf ears.

Lying became an everyday occurrence, and sometimes I would let her, because I didn't have it in me to fight. But, more and more, I saw her becoming dark, and I knew that if we didn't step in, she would be lost for good.

Our worry turned to panic when we learned that some of her boyfriend's roommates were doing drugs. This was a line we were not willing to let her cross. Brian, Doug, and I joined forces and forbade her from going to his house again.

"You can go to the movies, get coffee, or go out to dinner, but you cannot go to his house," we warned.

She nodded in agreement, but I was left with a gnawing pit in my stomach. Shortly after putting the rule into effect, Doug and I followed her when she said was going to the park to meet him.

We waited about a half an hour and drove to his house. When we arrived, she was there. I took her keys and put her in the car with Doug, forcing her to go home. The fight ensued but I had finally had enough. If she was going to continue to make poor decisions, she was now going to have to do it without my help.

I had done everything I could to try to keep our relationship secure, but it had become clear that I now had to be willing to let her fail — even if it meant that she would run away with him. I could not look myself in the mirror knowing I had not done everything I could to save her. And saving her might mean that I would have to temporarily lose her.

"You want to be on your own?" I challenged when we got home. "You are officially on your own. You now have no car, no money, no television, no computer, and you have no phone," I said taking her cell phone from her hand. "You are going to your father's, and you are staying there until break is over." Luckily, it was Fall Break, and she was going to be out of school for several days. She glared at me, daring me to keep my word.

"I have spent the past year and a half making decisions out of fear that you would run off and marry him. Well, you just go ahead and marry him, Brea," I ranted. "If you want to ruin your life, do it — but you will get no help from me."

"I don't want to marry him!" she screamed.

That was good news to me, or it would have been, had I believed her. I didn't.

"You are sick of living with us?" I parroted. "Fine, the moment you turn eighteen, you are out of here. I never thought I would say this. I never thought I could say this, but I am sick of you, Brealyn. You don't care who you hurt, and you don't care who you are turning into. So go, be on your own!" I yelled.

My heart broke as I heard myself say those words to her. How could I say them, much less feel them? She had been my whole life since the day she got here.

But I did mean them, and that hurt me worse than any mastectomy or hip revision ever could.

Her eyes became as big as saucers, and she started to back down. "What about college? How am I going to pay for that?" Her tone became softer as the consequences of her actions started to sink in.

"I don't know and I don't care," I said, shaking my head. "But you will not get one dime from me. I'm done. Now get packed."

She reluctantly gathered her things, and for the first time in my life, I drove her to her father's, not counting the moments until her return.

Chapter Forty-Eight
The Prodigal Daughter

During the hip revision, the stress was so close to overtaking me that I could smell it. When my father died, it lived on my chest waiting for the perfect moment to consume me. It felt like its patience was finally being rewarded, and the moment for its victory was here. I had to escape, because if I didn't, depression would finally call my body home.

I spent the next day on the Internet looking at places to get away so I wouldn't be home when Brea got back.

"Go, do what you need to do," Doug said, knowing that he was close to witnessing my final demise. "I'll take care of her. Get out of here before it's too late."

Brian called later that night. "I think she's turned a corner," he said hopefully.

I didn't believe it for a minute and continued to make plans to leave. I had already seen all her tricks. She was a master at telling you what you wanted to hear.

"Don't let her fool you," I warned. "She's not sincere."

"I really think she is," he replied, relating how she had just chastised her younger sister for speaking hatefully to her mother — Brea's stepmother.

"I cannot believe she thinks it's okay to talk that way to Sheilla," Brea told her dad.

"You mean exactly the way you've been talking to your mother?" Brian retorted.

"She got this look on her face like she was in shock," he told me. "I could see it in her eyes; she didn't realize what she was doing, Stacy," he tried to convince me.

"I simply don't believe her," I told him, "and I just can't take it anymore. I don't have it in me. If you're so convinced, let her move in with you," I said, wanting him to realize he was far from having her "fixed."

"Just give me the rest of the weekend," he consoled. "Let me spend some time with her and get her to see what she's doing."

"Good luck with that," I said sarcastically and hung up.

Saturday, I was still online looking at flights and bed and breakfasts in Savannah, Georgia. I wasn't going to tell Brealyn or her dad that I was leaving. Doug would be meeting Brian to pick her up, and he could let them know. I didn't want her to feel as if I were abandoning her, but I knew I couldn't face one more confrontation with her, or I might do something I would regret.

The phone rang.

"You're not going to believe this," Brian said. "I think we have our daughter back."

I was shaking my head "no" when I realized he couldn't see me. "She's telling you what you want to hear," I preached. "She lies. That is all she has been doing for months. She's doing it now," I warned him again.

"I really don't think she is," he sounded sincere.

He told me they had spent hours talking about her life: who she used to be and who she wanted to become. They talked of the hopes and dreams that the grandparents who had passed on, and those who still remained, had for her. They spoke of the reason she was here on the Earth. He plied her with story after story of the love that had freely been given to her and sacrifices that had been made for her.

"I think she finally gets it," he said wearily. "Just give her one more chance. I will make sure she knows it is her last, but don't give up on her now."

I cried. My head told me not to believe it, but my heart screamed for me to. I canceled my plans to leave town and with great trepidation. I met them on Sunday and brought her home.

"I'm so sorry," she cried when she saw me, tears streaming down her face. "I know you don't trust me," she continued "but I'm going to prove it to you. I don't want to be like this," she continued sobbing.

As we began our drive home, she sat next to me quietly. Finally, she spoke again.

"I don't know why I lie," she almost whispered. "I think it's unconscious, and I'm just so used to it now that I don't even think about it." I could tell this was a newfound realization on her part, one that she was just processing.

Even though they were the exact words I had longed to hear, I still hesitated to believe them. I couldn't afford to. I tried to respond without emotion. I was too fragile to let myself get sucked in again.

"I hope you mean what you say, Brealyn. I never in my wildest dreams thought we would be in this place. Your dad, Sheilla, Doug, and I have done everything we could to give you the most amazing life anyone could have, and you spit on us," I paused, letting my words take hold. "I really hope you mean it, but I'm not just going to believe you. You have to earn back our trust," I looked at her, searching her face to see if she understood that I was serious.

"I know," she said, lowering her head. "I'm going to. I promise."

For several months, she remained without a car, phone, television, and all the other luxuries she had been accorded. She called it "Living Amish." She also asked me to set her up in counseling with Elaine, and she attended each week.

Day by day, truth by truth, she did what she said she was going to do. She earned our trust, and ever so slowly, we did indeed get our daughter back.

Chapter Forty-Nine
Stop Thinking and Start Thanking

Even with Brea's troubles behind us, I couldn't shake the anxiety when I had to leave the house. Depression had been a problem for my father, and twice in my life, I had succumbed to its icy fingers.

The first time, I had been young. I was twenty-two and didn't understand what it was or how to help myself. I rode it out, although not too successfully.

The second time, I was almost thirty, newly divorced and a single mom. That time, because my father had spoken with me about it, I understood it more, although I didn't know I could get help for it. Again, I rode it out, waiting for the blackness to give way to light. It took over a year.

Now, however, I knew what I was facing, and I made a

conscious decision that I was not going to let it reside with me again. I understood that some depression was normal, considering what I had been through, and that was okay. What wasn't okay with me was to let it consume me as it had before. I had too much to do and too many people relying on me, and staying locked in my home was not something I could do.

When I got in the car, the sadness would plant itself next to me. I can't explain it other than to say it was much like the gut feeling you get when you are in danger. It was uncomfortable and caused wariness and a heightened sense of dread. With each day's passage, it was becoming worse. I had to force myself to get into my car and make the necessary trips to keep our home running. By the time I made it home, my head would be pounding from the tenseness in my body.

One blustery winter day, knowing that snow was on its way and I needed to restock on groceries, I made myself drive the two-mile trip to the supermarket. Halfway there, I started having trouble breathing, and because I was in the middle of construction, I couldn't pull over and stop. Something whispered to me: *stop thinking about it, and start being thankful instead.*

I did.

I focused on the sky, thanking God for its beauty. Then I noticed a road construction worker smiling as I drove past. I sent a halfhearted smile back and thanked God for the man's act of kindness. I began looking around to absorb whatever beauty or kindness I could find.

Before I knew it, I was at the store, and I was completely relaxed. I repeated the practice on my way home, and for the first time in several months, I felt like my old self.

I wish I could say I was cured, but I wasn't. The "Stop Thinking and Start Thanking" routine had to become a part of my life every day, and it is still a part that I cannot live without.

However, I'm not complaining. It has made a wonderful difference and awakened me to gifts that I have always taken for granted. Even when I no longer need to, it will remain a part of my life.

Chapter Fifty
It's Over

December came, and it was finally time to have the last part of my reconstructive surgery, the areola tattoos. I had never gotten a tattoo, but I had seen it done on television. I didn't want any part of the needle, but I told myself it was the means to an end — a very good and much anticipated end.

A slender nurse in brown scrubs with shoulder-length blond hair and a warm and lovely smile greeted me. She took my hand in both of hers and looked me in the eye. I could tell she had done this many times before.

"It's a happy day," she said, smiling. I forced a small smile, because it took me a moment to understand.

"It's almost over," she added. "This is your last procedure."

"Yes, thankfully," I managed; but somehow, my mood didn't match hers. More than anything, I wanted to believe that this was almost over; but the never-ending barrage I had been through had left a deep scar on my soul. Each time I thought my burdens were finished, another one seemed to show up, every new one trying to top the last.

I wasn't willing to let my guard down enough to completely believe this was the end, because if I did and one more thing happened to me, I knew I was going to lose it. I felt as if I had to protect my psyche the way a mother bear protects her cubs.

The nurse led me to a room and had me sit in a procedure chair. "I just want to walk you through what's going to happen," she said with the same warm smile on her face.

She told me of the tattooing process; we talked about the color I wanted for the nipples and the areolas and what kind of pain would be involved. I felt my chest tightening at the thought. I told her that unlike most of her patients, my nerve endings had grown back so I could feel everything.

Because my body and my psyche had been stretched to their absolute limits after the hip prosthesis broke, I felt as if I could not endure so much as a pinprick. I felt like I would finally break.

She assured me that she would make the procedure as painless as possible. I began breathing again. She led me back to the waiting area and again clasped both of my hands. "I'll take good care of you," she promised.

I scheduled the procedure for the following week. I decided to be proactive about the pain, so I took some leftover pain medication before I went. I asked Laura to drive me to the appointment.

I sat in the waiting area until the same nurse retrieved me. Again, she was smiling. "I bet you are happy to get this over," she said as she led me to her procedure room.

I nodded. She gave me a smock and told me to take off my blouse. "I'll be back in just a moment and we'll get started," she said as she closed the door and left me to undress.

She returned in about five minutes. "Okay, let's get started," she said. She reclined the chair and was now looking me in the eye. "It's been a long road, hasn't it?"

My throat began to tighten. *"Oh my God,"* I thought to myself. *"This has been the longest road of my life"* — and the tears began to flow.

"I'm so sorry," I said, dabbing my eyes with my fingertips.

She quickly grabbed some tissue and handed it to me.

"Don't you apologize," she comforted. "It's okay. You have been through so much. I can't even imagine. It's okay to cry. Please don't feel bad."

It was hard for me to stop. I wasn't sobbing — just leaking — but I couldn't control it.

"I'm okay," I assured her. "It just really has been a long road. I'm embarrassed that I'm acting like this. I know everything's going to be okay. It's just hard..."

She grabbed my hand again. "Can I pray for you?" she asked. I nodded yes and closed my eyes.

She asked that God be with me during the procedure and that he give me peace. I continued leaking. "Are you ready?"

she questioned. I nodded again.

She gave me several shots of novocain around the nipple and skin that she would tattoo. The tattooing machine made a buzzing noise as she began the process. I could feel the little pinprick sensations. They were slightly uncomfortable, but tolerable. Occasionally, she would hit a spot that had not been deadened. I would jump, and she would give me another shot. I chose to look at the ceiling instead of all the blood that she continued dabbing from my chest.

About three hours later, she was finished. I stood up and looked into a mirror on her wall. Although they were bright red and oozing, they were two of the most beautiful sights I had ever seen. I looked like a real woman again and not some science project gone wrong.

I was speechless. It had been so long since I had seen anything on my chest that looked that normal. Again, I cried. It was over. It was finally over.

The next couple of weeks went by, and the scabbing on my breasts disappeared. I would look at myself in the mirror and sigh. It was a feeling of contentment that I hadn't known in almost three years.

I loved the way I looked. I showed them off to my husband every time he was around. I asked him what he thought, and he would smile, a real and genuine smile of approval. "I love them, sweetheart," he said. "They are gorgeous" — and I could tell he meant it.

Chapter Fifty-One
Life Lessons

Sometimes we feel abandoned by God. We can't see Him, we can't hear Him, and most importantly, we can't feel Him. What I've learned is that He is everywhere, and there was no abandonment — quite the contrary.

During my journey, I received a quantity of love I didn't know existed — more than most people receive in a lifetime. My soul was nurtured and my body hugged — hugged not only by those I knew, but also perfect strangers.

What I came to realize is that every one of those hugs was from God — they were just delivered through His children.

He sent comforts in the form of a husband who wouldn't let me see myself as anything other than beautiful, letters of encouragement from people I had never met, home-cooked meals from family and friends, a pair of fuzzy white socks, amazing photographs of His creations, and a beautiful dog named Maxwell. All of these things were filled with His love.

I learned that with commitment and the realization of what is really important in life, a broken relationship can turn into a perfect love.

I learned that we cannot begin to understand why people are the way they are until we have walked through their hell.

I learned that even in death, those we love can teach us things they were not able to teach in life.

The last months with my father enabled me to see the soul behind the man. It gave me a newfound appreciation for his sacrifices, his pain, and his fragility. And it taught me that often our judgments are simply erroneous, because we haven't been given the whole picture.

Through his example, my father also taught me that the three most powerful words in the English language are "I am sorry." Those words allowed me to move beyond the past and rebuild a wonderful relationship that I never would have had with him.

I learned that every time you think you can't endure one more harsh moment in your life, you can, and you will, if you walk among friends.

I learned that life is filled with mountaintops and valleys, and every valley you walk through will make each mountaintop view more breathtaking.

I learned that there really are angels on earth, and they are not the celestial kind. They are ordinary people whose only wish is to walk beside you and pick you back up when you fall.

I learned that even if a thousand tears have been shed, they may not be enough, and the best thing to do is let them come.

I learned that sometimes decisions seem too insurmountable to make on our own, but we must. Although the task seems impossible, we are not alone. Each of us possesses a still, small voice that beckons to be heard. It is a voice that will never lead you astray, but you must learn to hear it.

I learned that any decision made out of fear will always be the wrong decision. We have to walk ourselves through those fears, seeing them from the other side for what they really are — illusions.

I learned that when you are not feeling heard; you must give yourself permission to speak louder. Because I did that, both my doctor and I were better for it. We became a team, working together to get me through the rest of my surgeries. She is now one of my heroes.

Finally, I learned that every day has a blessing waiting to be acknowledged — it's all about our perspective. We can either spend our time focusing on the bad — "thinking" — or we can spend it seeking the good — "thanking." Life may indeed bring with it much pain and suffering, but if one just opens their eyes, there is beauty in every direction beckoning us to drink from its source. "Every time we remember to say 'thank you,' we experience nothing less than Heaven on Earth." -- Sarah Ban Breathnach

The journey I made let me see God in all His glory — because He provided me with everything I needed to make it, and He sent me a guardian for the trip — Crazy Woman.

She has become less and less a part of my life, and the farther I am removed from the trauma, the meeker she becomes. Still, she appears from time to time when I am having a vulnerable moment.

I am more comfortable in my own skin now, but there is still the knowledge that I am not whole. Some days while I am exercising, I will catch a glimpse of myself in the mirror. It's not my face that I see. My chest dominates my body.

My breasts are much larger than my real ones had been. I have very broad shoulders and a wide chest wall; and to compensate, the implants are about a "D" cup in width, although they are only a "B" cup in projection.

She will tell me how hideous they are. I buy into it, because I know they are not me, and I am self-conscious about their size. I want them to be inconspicuous, but they are not. She knows that about me and uses it.

Sometimes she is able to wreak havoc on my psyche, and I will go to Doug, complaining about the way I look.

He is always supportive.

"They are beautiful," he will say, and then he grabs me by the shoulders, making me look into his eyes.

"They are beautiful," he whispers, "and you are still here. That is all that matters."

I have come to realize that my leg will never be the same either. It is difficult for me to sit comfortably for any length of time. I limp, and some days, I have pains that leave me stranded in mid-step, unable to walk. Those are the times I feel her bubble to the surface, ready to attack anyone that gets in her way.

Although most of what she tried to make me believe was indeed crazy, she served a purpose. She was my protector at a time when I was not able to protect myself. She was the guardian that kept the wolves at bay. She was the devil's advocate that made me see what I was too weak and afraid to see. But, I don't need her anymore — not really.

My plan is to let sleeping dogs lie — to tiptoe through what's left of my life with joy in my heart and a prayer on my tongue that — as useful as she was — I will never need her again.

Epilogue

One of the greatest lessons I learned during my journey through cancer was how to help others who have faced the same scenario. I also learned how I couldn't help them. I want to share with you that same insight in the hope that you may also help anyone you know who is battling a life-threatening disease.

These tips may not be beneficial in all situations, but I think most are universal. Here is a list of Do's and Don'ts.

Do: Tell the person you are thinking of them and praying for them. Because, honestly, it is the only thing you can do to really help.

Do: Offer your services to drive to doctors' appointments or help with errands. They may not take you up on it, but I know for me, there were times that I would not have been able to make it without the help of my friends who unselfishly drove me to appointments, took my child to and from school, brought meals, and sent words of encouragement.

Don't: Tell them about other people you know who have cancer. I can't stress this enough. I was not able to wrap my mind around my own cancer, much less muster sympathy for someone else with it. It was awkward and disheartening to hear about it. That may seem insensitive, but it is not. I could not think normally during that time, and it made me feel hopeless.

Don't: Bombard them with information that you've found about their disease. Most times, because of the fear, I was not able to process what my doctors were telling me. There was no way I could process all the magazine and newspaper articles about cancer or newest "studies" my friends had heard about.

I want to note, however, I totally understand why people wanted to give me the information.

When you find out someone you care about is facing a life-threatening disease, it leaves you feeling completely helpless, when all you want to do is help. It is a small way of feeling like you are helping and not leaving yourself so isolated.

Do: Support whatever decision they make regarding their health care. Sometimes it is extremely hard to watch someone you love make what you consider to be the "wrong" decision. But you have to understand that those decisions didn't come without due consideration and, sometimes, absolute agony.

It took me over four months to make a decision regarding my own care. I had no knowledge of what I was going to go through with a bilateral mastectomy, because no one had prepared me. During the reconstruction process, there were many times, because of the pain involved, that I questioned what I had done. But looking back on it now and knowing what I know, it may have not been right for others, but I am completely sure I did the right thing for me, and I have no regrets. I would do it all again.

Don't: Tell them what *you* would do, because the fact is, you don't really know unless you have already been there.

It was like a dagger through my heart when one of my friends and one of my family members told me, "Well, that's not what I would have done." I know the statement was made out of ignorance, but it didn't soften the blow.

Again, you have no idea what you would really do unless you walk yourself through every possible scenario of what a treatment plan may or may not mean for you.

Please do not be insensitive when someone who has done that finally makes the decision that is right for them.

Don't: Forget the caregiver. Caregivers are going through everything the patient is, and sometimes more. I still cannot comprehend how my husband got through it all. Dealing with my physical and emotional needs left little or no time for him to handle his own. He needed the same support system as I needed.

Caregivers need to vent. They need to cry, they need to process, and they need someone who will let them do that. They have such a horrible dilemma, because if they show that they are mad, tired, upset, or frustrated, they may be perceived as uncaring or unsupportive. They are not. They are only human and need a safe shoulder upon which to lean.

Please offer to be that support for them.

Don't: Let the diagnosis change the way you act around your loved one. More than anything else, I needed something to be ordinary in my life. I needed a safe place where nothing had changed. If you lunch with your girlfriends every week and rag on your husbands, then by all means, continue to do that. Don't let your topic of conversation turn to the disease. Keep everything exactly as it was before.

Don't: Be afraid to ask if your loved one wants to talk about it when the time and place is right. And, at the same time, don't be offended if they don't. My mood was like an ocean tide. One day, I would come in and need someone to lean on. The next day, I would retreat, needing to go inside and make sense of things on my own.

Do: Offer to get them in touch with someone you know who has already been through the disease (not someone currently going through it). And, again, do not be offended if they don't take you up on it.

Right after my initial diagnosis, my sister made an offer to get me in touch with a friend of hers who had been though it, but I couldn't contact her. Again, my edges were too raw, and I didn't know if I was coming or going.

After the second diagnosis, however, another friend of mine made the same offer. I jumped on it and called the woman within five minutes, because I was at a point where I needed to be able to see the disease from the other side. It's all a matter of timing. Just to let your loved one know that option is available is enough.

Do: Laugh. Laugh long and laugh hard, and don't feel guilty about it. In fact, do everything you can to help your loved one laugh. Take them to funny movies, tell them jokes, act stupid and crazy together. The endorphins released in laughter are a thousand times more powerful than the best cancer drugs available. It's a proven fact.

Do: Be cognizant of your conversation. What I mean is, don't harp on how upset you are about your favorite team losing a football game, or how the lady in the supermarket checkout treated you.

I was overly sensitive during that time, and when people talked about things like that, it made me cringe. To a cancer patient, those things are insignificant and petty when they are or may be dying.

I know I was not in the right about this. I was just overly sensitive. The point is, be aware of what may really be important and what isn't.

Do: Let the person be whatever they need to be at any given time. If they need to pretend it isn't happening, pretend with them. If they need to complain, join in. If they need to cry, cry too. Take your cue from them, and *let them be*. You cannot change their mood. In fact, you will make it worse.

They need to know that whatever they have to go through emotionally is okay. And more than that, they need to know you "get it." Trying to change their mood means you don't, and it sends the message that how they feel isn't okay when, in fact, it's exactly as it should be.

Finally and most importantly: Let Go and Let God. There is nothing you can do to change the circumstances. Each of us must walk our own path, and it is not for others to question what path that may be.

My journey through cancer was one of the greatest gifts of my lifetime. It gave me new eyes with which to see what really exists in the world. I wouldn't trade it for anything.

God Bless each of you on your own journey. May your gift, in whatever form it is given, awaken you to all the love and beauty you may have been missing along the way.

Stacy

Acknowledgments

First, I want to thank my family, Douglas, Brealyn, and Oliver, for your love and support, not only during my illness, but during our lives together. Because of you, I am blessed.

This book would not have been possible without the support and guidance of my friend and mentor, Bob Burg. You are an amazing Go-Giver and person. To my dear friend Svetlana Kim, thank you for your encouragement and support of this project. You are an inspiration. To Heidi Richards Mooney and Libby Gill, thank you for wading through the manuscript and your invaluable input. You are amazing women and leaders. I can only aspire to your greatness. To Sanjiv Goyal, thank you for your unbelievable generosity. It is unmatched. Thank you to Tarun Vishnoi for all your help with the book's website and to Brian Brashier for your technical assistance with the cover design.

To my friends Kathy McIver and Angie Kerschen, thank you for being two of my first readers and for your editing suggestions. Most importantly, thank you for being the amazing friends and support systems you have been.

Thank you to the family that supported me during my illness, including the entire Shelton family, especially my mother-in-law, Barbara; my siblings, especially my sister, Cheryl Gurley; and my mother.

To my amazing and giving friends, Laura Ingram, Pam Voss, Pam Hooper, Lisa Todd, Karin Monk, Ann Harris, Jenny Ladner, Brett and Eileen Husserl, Kim Sanborn, Ray James, Barbara Young, Monica Klima, Judy Clayton, Cristie Hughes, Tammy Higginbotham, and the ladies of Arbonne: words cannot begin to express what you have meant to me. "Thank you" will never be enough.

I want to thank my incredible surgeons. I believe they are three of the most gifted physicians in the country. Thank you to Dr. William Harris and Dr. James Monk for going above and beyond in caring for me and to Dr. Leslie Ollar-Shoemake for giving me the courage to do what I needed to do. I believe her willingness to speak frankly with me saved my life. To all the nurses and support staff who helped in my recovery, thank you for devoting your lives to the care and well-being of others. And to Dr. Misty Hsieh, thank you for restoring my daughter to good health.

In loving memory of my wonderful grandparents and guardian angels, Glenn and Lithia Brewer and Maude DePrater, and my newest angel, my father, Billy L. DePrater.

Finally, to Maxwell "Buppy" Shelton, you are the greatest of dogs.

About the Author

Stacy D. Shelton is a former award-winning broadcast and print journalist. She now speaks publicly about her journey through cancer and the life lessons that remained. She also counsels families, patients, and survivors on dealing with life-threatening diseases. She is a CASA and a BRIDGES volunteer.

She lives in Oklahoma with her husband, Doug; daughter, Brealyn; and their dogs, Max and Teddy.

Ms. Shelton has become active in the Susan G. Komen Race for the Cure and now embraces her pink ribbon status.

To contact her, inquire about speaking engagements, or purchase additional copies of this book, visit her website at http://www.StacyDShelton.com.